EQUIP

THE KINGDOM STORY
E X P E R I E N C E

SMALL GROUP STUDY

OLD TESTAMENT

DR. JOHN S. LEWIS

THE KINGDOM STORY EXPERIENCE
SMALL GROUP STUDY
THE OLD TESTAMENT

ISBN: 979-8-9871352-9-7

Primary Editorial: Arlyn Lawrence, Inspira Literary Solutions, Gig Harbor, WA

Book Design: Kami Wright, inMode Design, Maple Valley, WA. Illustrations: Adobe Stock

Printed in the USA by Ingram Spark, Nashville, TN

Additional books from EQUIP and John S. Lewis

The Kingdom Story Experience — Small Group Study — The New Testament Story

Discipleship Reframed — Building a Framework for a Culture of Disciple-Making

Three Nails, One Purpose — Following Christ to His Cross and Resurrection

Finding the Treasure in Christmas — Advent Traditions for Families with Kids of All Ages

*This book is dedicated to Kingdom Story alumni
who patiently helped me discover the wings of story in my
own stony heart, and to the King of Kings, whose fingerprints
I can see from cover to cover, and who, in the words of a
famous rabbi, created you and me because...*
God loves story.

TABLE OF CONTENTS

Foreword...ii

Introduction...iii

Our Approach and Goals..iii

The Elements..iv

LESSON 1 | GENESIS 2:4-25
We Are Created from Dust to Life.. 1

LESSON 2 | GENESIS 3
Sin Shuts Out Eden's Glory..11

LESSON 3 | GENESIS 12:1-5
God Blesses Abram...21

LESSON 4 | EXODUS 20:1-17
God Commands His People to Love..29

LESSON 5 | NUMBERS 13:25-14:11
Twelve Spies and Two Types of Fear...37

LESSON 6 | JUDGES 2:6-23
Israel in Bondage to Idolatry..47

LESSON 7 | 1 SAMUEL 16:1-13
A King Is Chosen for Israel..57

LESSON 8 | 1 KINGS 18:17-42
Elijah Brings the Fire of God...67

LESSON 9 | JEREMIAH 29:1-14
Jeremiah Brings God's Hope to Babylon..77

LESSON 10 | NEHEMIAH SELECTIONS
The Rebuilding of Jerusalem's Walls...85

The Ups and Downs of God's Kingdom Story Diagram 95

Acknowledgments 96

FOREWORD

As a pastor of a church in the first quarter of the 21st century, I have come to this regrettable conclusion: we live in a time where a significant part of Christianity in the United States is only tenuously Christian. Most self-identified Christians are disconnected from the historical tradition of faith, having exchanged the fullness of Kingdom living for (at best) an hour on Sunday. Instead of robust faith in Jesus, many settle for a pale watered-down version of the Kingdom in which Jesus invites us to participate. As a result, the Church today is in crisis.

Much of this crisis comes from a lack of Biblical foundations and transformation, which in turn has created a leadership crisis. There are many reasons why we find ourselves in this place, but among all the remedies I've experienced or explored, none hold the power of The Kingdom Story.

How do I know? Because God used *The Kingdom Story Experience* to rescue me from the kind of nominal faith that is so common today. I grew up going to church with my family, which is to say we attended weekly services and, depending on the congregation, participated in Sunday school and youth groups. As such, I knew a lot about the Bible and the classic stories that hold the imagination of an adolescent. But all those stories seemed anchored only to the past.

It wasn't until my late college years that I began to understand what it meant to have a living relationship with Christ, specifically that the Kingdom of God wasn't bound to people who lived the stories of the Bible. Rather, the Kingdom of God is a story that we are continually invited into. It is a "Kingdom" story— and it's all around us. It would be no overstatement to say that *The Kingdom Story Experience* was for me, at 23 years old, one of the most formative exercises in my faith journey.

I was serving in a parachurch youth ministry, passionate about sharing the love of Jesus, but I struggled to hold a coherent theology or integrated biblical perspective on so many issues. Where the Bible had before seemed to be just a collection of disparate stories and genres, this body of work helped me develop a holistic understanding of Scripture and then integrate my heart and head with my hands and habits. I was led to see both my ministry and my city in a new way.

When I came on staff at University Place Presbyterian Church (UPPC), I began to see the necessity of such training among our staff, younger interns, and volunteer leaders. Starting in the 1990s, from the youth department to our church at large, I have witnessed God use *The Kingdom Story Experience* with all sorts of men, women, and young people to bring life to their part in God's story.

Because the teaching connects with real world implications, participants experience the beautiful symmetry of growing in love with God while experiencing the desire to love and serve others.

I am now Senior Pastor at UPPC, and now more than ever I am convinced we need this approach toward spiritual and vocational formation. This is a resource that many churches could benefit from just as it has at UPPC.

John's leadership and writing is a treasure, and I am excited for you to know the transformation that comes with this sort of experience. *You will be forever changed because of it!*

REV. AARON STEWART
SENIOR PASTOR
UNIVERSITY PLACE PRESBYTERIAN CHURCH
UNIVERSITY PLACE, WASHINGTON

Introduction

The concept of viewing the Bible as a coherent, overarching story has gained momentum in Western Christianity, and for good reason. Stories have a unique power to captivate, helping us learn, grow, and remember. However, despite the common focus on reading and hearing scripture, there is a need for resources that deeply root believers in *discipleship* and *understanding* of God's larger, biblical story.

Since 1994, the *Kingdom Story Experience (KSE)* has aimed to fulfill this need by immersing participants in God's bigger story. Its core mission is to let the Lord's story shape lives, using the power of storytelling to create faithful disciples of Jesus. The KSE helps participants engage with the Bible not only as a text but as a *dynamic adventure*, one that influences how they live out their faith in their homes, workplaces, and communities.

This study has proven to be transformative for hundreds of participants, year after year, giving them a new (or renewed) sense of confidence and a strong faith foundation. It is more impactful when led by a facilitator and shared with at least three other participants. When these elements are in place, something very special happens. The experience becomes even more impactful, as each person's unique story contributes to a shared process of connecting with God's story. This communal aspect fosters a genuine, sometimes messy, yet deeply meaningful process. *We believe your experience with God's Kingdom Story will be unforgettable!*

Our Approach and Goals

The Bible is a rich, interconnected story, yet its complexity often makes it challenging to grasp—whether you're new to it or have been reading it for years. The KSE will guide you through key lessons carefully chosen for their historical significance and ability to illuminate the bigger picture. These stories serve like the edge pieces of a jigsaw puzzle, helping you piece together the framework of God's grand narrative and see how each part connects to reveal the fuller picture.

As you go forward, keep a few things in mind:

► Theologically, we aim to be Christ-centered and faithful to historic Christian orthodoxy, embracing the paradoxes and tensions of truth.

► Many hold misguided views of the Bible that weaken people's understanding of God and the Christian life. We believe that understanding God's full story arc can bring healing and clarity to these misperceptions.

► People across all cultures are captivated by stories. Our approach taps into emotions and life thoughts that simple principles and fill-in-the-blank answers cannot. We encourage and facilitate participants to step into the biblical characters' shoes and also share their own challenges or insights.

► The left (logical) and right (imaginative) sides of the brain are equally engaged during a story. Our imaginations are sparked, desires are stirred, and our ability to remember what we learn is enhanced. When this happens, our comprehension and conviction increase.

► The facilitator's role is to guide participation and vulnerability, but keep the focus on Jesus, not human ability or our behavior. Our view of faith, responsibility, and grace is enlarged when God is the hero of each story. We take God more seriously and ourselves less. This is freedom!

The Lesson Elements

Each lesson element is briefly explained below, providing participants and facilitators with a foundational overview of the purpose behind each section.

HEADER PANEL

Lessons begin with two stated purposes, a memory verse, the kingdom theme, a discipleship practice, and a prayer. While the Holy Spirit will lead participants beyond these parameters, they set the direction.

INTRODUCTION

This section provides a review of the last lesson's story and a glimpse into the next story. It also introduces the next theme and begins to connect it to our own current story.

WHAT IS YOUR EXPERIENCE?

One or two questions are offered for participants to share personal experiences related to the theme, helping prepare us to engage with the Bible passage with personal connections in mind.

THE BIGGER STORY

A specific parallel passage shows how a given story connects to other instances within the broader narrative of the Bible.

EXPLORE THE STORY

Participants will be assigned a character and explore the story through that lens. Certain characters are always considered:

► *Evil:* **the antagonist, the Devil,** who is always tempting, lying, and infiltrating culture and systems, constantly at odds with the advancement of God's Kingdom

► *Human characters:* **individuals or groups** who are actively or indirectly involved in the story

► *God:* **the hero protagonist** who is always God-Father, Son, or Holy Spirit

LIVE INTO THE STORY

This section offers options for discussion, personal reflection, action, and prayer. These four activities help participants connect God's character to their own stories and discover their place in His greater narrative:

- ▶ **God the Hero**—Exploring what we learned about God.

- ▶ **Our Story**—Seeking how the lessons speak to our personal experience of God's story. This question often travels full circle and explores how the lesson's truths connect with the **What Is Your Experience** question earlier in the lesson.

- ▶ **Reaching Others**—Finding a practical and culturally relevant implication of the lesson toward love, service, or leadership of others.

LOOKING AHEAD

The lesson closes with a bridge toward what's next in the story arc.

THEORY TO PRACTICE: *RESPONSE FOR DISCIPLES*

- ▶ **Prayer Ideas**—Options for a prayer experience either at the lesson's end or afterwards on their own. The goal is to encourage the practice of prayer in the life of each participant.

- ▶ **Action Ideas**—Practical ideas for the week ahead. The goal is to act on what was learned in a relevant way as an integral part of discipleship.

- ▶ **Discipleship Practice**—A defined spiritual practice linked to the lesson's theme and an explanation of *why* this practice matters today.

THEN THE LORD GOD FORMED A MAN FROM THE DUST OF THE GROUND AND BREATHED INTO HIS NOSTRILS THE BREATH OF LIFE, AND THE MAN BECAME A LIVING BEING.

GENESIS 2:7

We Are Created From Dust to Life

GENESIS 2:4-25

PURPOSE

1. To better understand God's character and purpose for all he created.

2. To commit to experiencing life as God intended in all our relationships.

MEMORY VERSE

The Lord God commanded the man, *"Eat, eat from any tree in the garden; but you must not eat from the tree of the knowledge of good and evil, for when you eat from it you will die, die."* (Genesis 2:16-17) (Words doubled for emphasis in Hebrew)

KINGDOM THEME

Vision of God

DISCIPLESHIP PRACTICE

Time Stewardship

PRAYER

Creator God, we live in a world that has largely lost touch with your design for life. Please touch my eyes first to see you and your original, good purposes. Lead me with those I love to live into those purposes.

Introduction

Genesis 2, a profound continuation of Genesis 1, presents a second account of creation. Both narratives, in their unique ways, unveil the grandeur of everything in heaven and earth and illuminate God's character and eternal purpose.

This second, more informal creation story was likely shared by a religious leader with the gathered people or passed down by parents to their children.

In the Bible's creation stories, God reveals his perspective on the world and the purpose of our meaningful relationships with Him, each other, and creation. However, we often miss this because we view life through distorted lenses. Our choices and conditioning shape how we see the world, affecting every aspect of life for individuals and cultures alike.

As with Genesis 1, Genesis 2 addresses significant questions that help us navigate life and faith:

▶ *Who is God as our Creator?*

▶ *What does it mean for us that we are made from the earth's dust and in God's image?*

▶ *How are humans designed to relate to God, each other, and the created world?*

One of the most crucial questions for our lives is: *What is our vision of God?* Whether we are aware of it or not, our vision of God is the foundation of all we feel, think, do, and speak. Since the fall of Adam and Eve, humans tend to project onto God misperceptions that come from negative experiences. These 'glasses' for seeing God can cost us dearly.

The Genesis 1 and 2 creation stories focus on what God created and the dramatic introduction of a God worthy of our total trust. For example, God made the heavens and the earth *because God is* powerful (2:4). God created everything man and woman needed for flourishing (2:9-14) *because God is* a generous and trustworthy provider.

The creation of the garden and good fruit-bearing trees, the first command to eat from every tree in the garden, the creation of the woman out of the man's rib, and the delegating of the land and animals to their care—all these actions reveal God's supreme character.

Being created by this magnificent King comes with a profound responsibility. We are not just recipients of his love but also stewards of his creation. Our role is to love those around us and work in creation as responsible caretakers—nurturing God's plants, animals, and the environment.

As God's partners on earth, our work often becomes the primary way to live out this calling, including improving our community and shaping its culture. Our efforts can expand the influence of God's Spirit in our families, schools, workplace, media, religion, law, and government. The King uses our gifts and creativity in this process. Amazing!

What Is Your Experience?

Think of your life story as a sporting event. Circle several roles or positions God has often "played" in your "game" over the years. Give a brief example from your life for each choice. God is...

▸ A player out on the field, but I am the central player.

_____

▸ Only a spectator who watches me play from a distance.

_____

▸ A good coach on the sidelines who offers me advice, encouragement, and tips.

_____

▸ The referee who catches me making mistakes.

_____

▸ A second-string player, watching on the sidelines, waiting for a turn to come in.

_____

▸ The most valuable, game-winning player who also chooses me to be a player.

_____

Explore the Story

Consider the Viewpoints | Genesis 2:4-25

Your group leader will assign you a character below. Notice what your character does and says, and then imagine their thoughts and feelings. Share some of your discussion highlights, any lingering questions, and how you can possibly relate to this character.

GOD

God is Father, Son and Spirit, Creator, artist, sovereign and eternal King. He is revealing himself and unveiling his plans for us and the world.

THE WOMAN

She was created by God the "surgeon," by taking a rib from Adam's side. She completes the Man as his complement and companion.

MAN

He was created by God's breath out of the dust, given blessings and responsibilities and yet somehow still incomplete as the only human on earth.

Narrator

⁴ This is the account of the heavens and the earth when they were created, when the Lord God made the earth and the heavens. ⁵ Now no shrub had yet appeared on the earth and no plant had yet sprung up, for the Lord God had not sent rain on the earth and there was no one to work the ground, ⁶ but streams came up from the earth and watered the whole surface of the ground. ⁷ Then the Lord God formed a man from the dust of the ground and breathed into his nostrils the breath of life, and the man became a living being.

———————

⁸ Now the Lord God had planted a garden in the east, in Eden; and there he put the man he had formed. ⁹ The Lord God made all kinds of trees grow out of the ground—trees pleasing to the eye and good for food. In the middle of the garden was the Tree of Life and the Tree of the Knowledge of Good and Evil. ¹⁰ A river watering the garden flowed from Eden; from there, it was separated into four headwaters. ¹¹ The name of the first is the

(Scripture continues on the next page)

Pishon; it winds through the entire land of Havilah, where there is gold. ¹² *(The gold of that land is good; aromatic resin and onyx are also there.)* ¹³ *The name of the second river is the Gihon; it winds through the entire land of Cush.* ¹⁴ *The name of the third river is the Tigris; it runs along the east side of Ashur. And the fourth river is the Euphrates.* ¹⁵ *The Lord God took the man and put him in the Garden of Eden to work it and take care of it.*

---

¹⁶ *And the Lord God commanded the man,*

Lord God

"You are free to eat from any tree in the garden; ¹⁷ *but you must not eat from the tree of the knowledge of good and evil, for when you eat from it you will die. It is not good for the man to be alone.* ¹⁸ *I will make a helper suitable for him."*

Narrator

¹⁹ *Now the Lord God had formed out of the ground all the wild animals and all the birds in the sky. He brought them to the man to see what he would name them, and whatever the man called each living creature, that was its name.* ²⁰ *So the man gave names to all the livestock, the birds in the sky, and all the wild animals. But for Adam, no suitable helper was found.*

---

²¹ *So the Lord God caused the man to fall into a deep sleep; and while he was sleeping, he took one of the man's ribs and then closed up the place with flesh.* ²² *Then the Lord God made a woman from the rib he had taken out of the man, and he brought her to the man.*

The Man

23 "This is now bone of my bones and flesh of my flesh; she shall be called 'woman,' for she was taken out of man."

Narrator

24 That is why a man leaves his father and mother and is united to his wife, and they become one flesh.

25 Adam and his wife were both naked, and they felt no shame.

GENESIS 2:4-25

THE BIGGER STORY

Parallels of Jesus and the Genesis 1-2 Creation Stories

John 1:1-3, 14; Genesis 1 and 2	Summary from Genesis 2
God the Creator existed in the beginning.	Jesus was with God in the beginning.
God created the world by his powerful spoken word and actions.	Jesus is the Word of God; all things were created by him, and through him.
God created man, woman, and their union in his image.	Jesus as God took on human flesh so we could see in him the image of God.

 **Live into the Story**

God the Hero

God revealed himself as a *loving king and powerful creator* in this story—two important Biblical images. Make a short list of other traits you saw in God.

In this story, God is...

_____

_____

_____

_____

Our Story

Recall how you answered the question at the beginning of the lesson. How might Genesis 2 have challenged or expanded your vision of God and the role you want God to play in your life?

_____

_____

_____

_____

_____

Reaching Others

People spend over half of their lives working. God intended his stewards to express their creativity through work. Sadly, people's experience of work is often described as *frustrating, dead-end, meaningless, boring, overwhelming, manipulative, divisive, or unmotivating.* Give an example from a typical workplace where some of these descriptions apply.

_____

_____

Now, reimagine that work situation as if God was King and all of life was as he intended.

_____

_____

Looking Ahead

Many people struggle to see God as generous or to experience the fullness of life as he originally intended. To understand why this disconnect exists, we must look back to Genesis 3, where the tragic entrance of sin into the world disrupted humanity's relationship with God, each other, and creation itself.

Theory to Practice: *Response for Disciples*

Prayer Ideas

▸ Read Psalm 8 and reflect on God's wonderful creation, plan, and character revealed in this story. Afterward, take a moment to thank him for a specific aspect of creation that is especially meaningful to you.

▸ Recognize the intricate balance and design of creation—consider the marvel of the human body, the rhythm of day and night, the harmony of land and water, and the vast array of unique creatures that fill the sea, land, and sky.

▸ Spend a moment in gratitude, thanking God for the specific blessings he has placed in your life.

Action Ideas

▸ Walk in nature, at the beach, on a mountain, or at a local park. Be present with the God of creation and soak in his presence.

▸ Evaluate how you spend your time with this simple exercise. List 15 activities that take up most of your week and estimate how many hours you currently spend on each. Reflect on how much time you believe God would ideally have you devote to them. Compare the two columns and consider what adjustments could help you better align your priorities with God's best and steward your time more intentionally.

Discipleship Practice

▸ **Time Stewardship** | Time is God's and not ours. It is not ours to spend or to waste but rather to steward as we discern God's specific life priorities and set out to concentrate our will on those priorities. *Why?* To cultivate greater integrity, focus, confidence, and freedom to say *yes* and *no* as God's will dictates.

WHEN THE WOMAN SAW THAT THE FRUIT OF THE TREE WAS GOOD FOR FOOD AND PLEASING TO THE EYE, AND ALSO DESIRABLE FOR GAINING WISDOM, SHE TOOK SOME AND ATE IT.

GENESIS 3:6

Sin Shuts Out Eden's Glory

GENESIS 3

PURPOSE

1. To understand sin is more than breaking God's rules or doing something wrong; sin begins with our misperceptions of God and ourselves.

2. Commit to knowing God's character more clearly and then resist our flawed desire to be in charge.

MEMORY VERSE

Now the serpent was more crafty than any other of the wild animals that God had made. He said to the woman, 'Did God really say, "You must not eat from any tree of the garden?"' (Genesis 3:1)

KINGDOM THEME

Sin

DISCIPLESHIP PRACTICE

Financial Stewardship

PRAYER

God, open our eyes to see what is wrong with the world and our hearts. May our perceptions of sin and you be stretched by this tragic story.

Introduction

At the beginning of the Story (Genesis 2), God created man from the dust of the earth and breathed life into him. He then formed a woman from the man's side, placing them both in a lush, abundant garden. Their purpose was to work in the garden and enjoy its blessings.

God's simple command and expectation was that they keep him at the center of their life—a natural request from a holy King and loving Father.

One look at the world today tells us that much has changed since the Garden of Eden. What went wrong there? Genesis 3 records the Story's crisis.

In Eden, humans faced their first temptation, sin, and the painful consequences that followed. The crafty serpent planted a lie, leading the woman to see God as withholding and untrustworthy. Based on this faulty perception, the man and the woman pretended to be God. Believing they knew where to find true happiness, they ate from the forbidden tree.

But the serpent's "promise" failed them. Instead of becoming like God, sin stormed their peaceful world. Shame and blame, hiding from God, toiling in work, and disappointment in relationships—immediately ambushed their everyday lives.

Does any of this description of sin sound familiar?

Many of our world's problems can also be traced back to misperceptions of God. Though created in God's image, our sinful nature leads us to doubt God and trust ourselves.

The belief that we can run our own lives leads us to sinful rebellion and subsequent shame. We rely on our understanding of what will make us happy and loved. Disconnected from God and people, we end up lost and unhappy.

Whether viewing our family, school, workplace, or church, we all wear glasses that give us a warped view of God and his kingdom's purposes. This way of seeing moves us toward sin and its consequences. We hurt God, ourselves, and those we want to love.

We need deliverance…

What Is Your Experience?

Finish the following sentence using one or more of the options below: "When I find myself struggling and stuck in my pattern of sin, I often experience God as"…

- ▶ *Angry*
- ▶ *Distant*
- ▶ *Judging*
- ▶ *Unapproachable*
- ▶ *Disappointed*
- ▶ *Gracious*
- ▶ *Impatient*
- ▶ *Condemning*
- ▶ *Personal*
- ▶ *Lenient or Passive*
- ▶ *Other Misperceptions*

Explain your choice(s):

_____

_____

_____

_____

Explore the Story

Consider the Viewpoints | Genesis 3:1-24

After forming groups based on characters, explore the story together, reading and pausing in three sections: vv 1-7, vv. 8-13, vv. 14-25. Notice what your character does and says, and then imagine their accompanying thoughts and feelings. When you regather as a group, share some of your discussion highlights, any lingering questions, and how you can relate to this character.

THE SERPENT

The serpent's plan to corrupt Eden revolved around deceiving the woman and man into sin. In doing so, the serpent distorted their perception of God, forever changing the trajectory of their story, the entire biblical narrative, and our story today.

THE MAN

The Man should have come out of hiding and taken more responsibility to protect his new wife. Not only did he fail to do so, but he even blamed the Woman for his disobedience. His sin of silence preceded his eating the forbidden fruit. Passivity reigned in this tragic moment.

THE WOMAN

The Woman was susceptible to the serpent's misleading question about God's character. After eating the forbidden fruit and giving some to the Man, shame and blame arrived. These feelings and experiences were not at all what the serpent had promised.

GOD

Our Creator, the designer of paradise, loves his rebellious children. He is infinitely worthy of trust. When the serpent distorted God's worthy character, the man and woman fell into pride's trap of taking themselves too seriously.

Narrator

¹ Now the serpent was more crafty than any of the wild animals the Lord God had made.

The Serpent

"Did God really say, 'You must not eat from any tree in the garden'?"

The Woman

² "We may eat fruit from the trees in the garden,³ but God did say, 'You must not eat fruit from the tree that is in the middle of the garden, and you must not touch it, or you will die.'"

(Scripture continues on the next page.)

The Enemy

4 *"You will not certainly die, 5 for God knows that when you eat from it your eyes will be opened, and you will be like God, knowing good and evil."*

Narrator

6 *When the woman saw that the fruit of the tree was good for food and pleasing to the eye, and also desirable for gaining wisdom, she took some and ate it. She also gave some to her husband, who was with her, and he ate it. 7 Then the eyes of both of them were opened, and they realized they were naked; so, they sewed fig leaves together and made coverings for themselves.*

————————

8 *Then the man and his wife heard the sound of the Lord God as he was walking in the garden in the cool of the day, and they hid from the Lord God among the trees of the garden. 9 But the Lord God called to the man,*

Lord God to the Man

"Where are you?"

The Man

10 *"I heard you in the garden, and I was afraid because I was naked, so I hid."*

Lord God

11 *"Who told you that you were naked? Have you eaten from the tree that I commanded you not to eat from?"*

The Man

12 *"The woman you put here with me—she gave me some fruit from the tree, and I ate it."*

Lord God to the Woman

13 *"What is this you have done?"*

The Woman

"The serpent deceived me, and I ate."

————————

Lord God to the Serpent

¹⁴ "Because you have done this, "Cursed are you above all livestock and all wild animals! You will crawl on your belly, and you will eat dust all the days of your life. ¹⁵ And I will put enmity between you and the woman, and between your offspring and hers; he will crush your head, and you will strike his heel."

Lord God to the Woman

¹⁶ I will make your pains in childbearing very severe; with painful labor you will give birth to children. Your desire will be for your husband, and he will rule over you."

Lord God to the Man

¹⁷ "Because you listened to your wife and ate fruit from the tree about which I commanded you, 'You must not eat from it,' "Cursed is the ground because of you; through painful toil you will eat food from it all the days of your life. ¹⁸ It will produce thorns and thistles for you, and you will eat the plants of the field. ¹⁹ By the sweat of your brow, you will eat your food until you return to the ground, since from it you were taken; for dust you are and to dust you will return."

Narrator

²⁰ Adam named his wife Eve, because she would become the mother of all the living. ²¹ The Lord God made garments of skin for Adam and his wife and clothed them.

Lord God

²² "The man has now become like one of us, knowing good and evil. He must not be allowed to reach out his hand and take also from the tree of life and eat and live forever."

Narrator

²³ So the Lord God banished him from the Garden of Eden to work the ground from which he had been taken. ²⁴ After he drove the man out, he placed cherubim on the east side of the Garden of Eden and a flaming sword flashing back and forth to guard the way to the Tree of Life.

GENESIS 3:1-24

The Failure of Adam and Eve Contrasted with Jesus' Overcoming Temptation

Areas of Similarities and Differences	Adam and Eve in Eden (Genesis 3:1-7)	Jesus in the Wilderness (Matthew 4:1-11)
Before the temptation	God gave Eve blessings and a mission to rule. Adam and Eve are full of garden delights.	God gave Holy Spirit blessing and mission to be the Messiah. Jesus had been fasting 40 days.
Serpent tries to deepen deception and doubt	Serpent: "Did God really say… you will not die."	Serpent: "If you are the Son of God" and quotes scripture.
Their view of God	Adam and Eve lower their high view of God.	Jesus maintains a high view of God.
Their grounding in God's word	Eve misquotes God's commands and consequences.	Jesus quotes scripture by memory.
Temptation to "obey" feelings/desire	Adam and Eve cannot resist the temptation to "become like God," be self-centered, and eat the fruit for pleasure.	Jesus resists the temptation to turn stones to bread in his hunger or to jump off the heights to be praised.

 # Live into the Story

God the Hero

Throughout this story, God revealed himself as trustworthy, i.e., in a way opposite to the serpent's subtle attack in Genesis 3:1. Make a list of character traits you saw in God through his words and actions.

- ▶
- ▶
- ▶
- ▶
- ▶

Our Story

Summarize your insights from the first two lessons on God's vision for our lives by filling in the 3rd column.

Three key relationships of our lives in the Garden	Summary from Genesis 2	Examples of what stayed the same in Genesis 3 and what changed
Relationship of man and woman to *God*	Dependence on God's generous provision; willing submission and service to a good and powerful king; intimate communication and friendship.	What stayed the same: What changed:
Relationship of man and woman to *each other*	Man and woman are similar and yet differentiated from the animals. They need and complement each other, and are to procreating and steward the world together.	What stayed the same: What changed:
Relationship of man and woman to the *created world*	The created world provides for us, delights us, reflects God's character to us. We are to regularly enjoy and creatively steward it.	What stayed the same: What changed:

After comparing Eden's "before and after," how do you see life and sin here on earth differently?

Reaching Others

We have learned today that sin is rooted in a faulty view of God. From here follows the lie that Adam and Eve could live well independently. Knowing this could inform the way we approach and love people we know who are stuck in sin. What is one practical thing you could do to help others begin to recognize how they see and misperceive God?

_____

_____

_____

_____

Close Together in Prayer

Looking Ahead

The infection of sin begins in Genesis 3, and by the time we reach chapters 4 through 11, its destructive impact is unmistakable—corrupting hearts, relationships, and entire societies. Yet none of this took God by surprise. From the very beginning, he had a plan to restore his Kingdom on earth. In Genesis 12, we see the first unveiling of that redemptive promise—a foundational moment we'll explore in depth in our next lesson.

Theory to Practice: *Response for Disciples*

Prayer Ideas

▸ Pick a time and place where you can take a few minutes to leave people and activities to come to God alone. Ask God for forgiveness for the distorted way you see God. Try to do this several days in the week ahead.

▸ Read Psalm 32:1-7. Afterwards, lift up a prayer of thanksgiving that God's mercy is stronger than our rebellion.

Action Ideas

▸ Begin a short "Dear God" letter with, "God my Father, I admit…" and finish this sentence by bringing to God a pattern of sin in your life. Then read Genesis 3:1-7 and imagine yourself as either Adam or Eve. Add another sentence to your letter about how you find yourself like Adam or Eve in this story. Ask the God who walks toward you in the cool of the day for forgiveness.

▸ Reflect on your financial habits with this exercise. Create a page with three columns to evaluate your spending and saving. In the first column, list your top 15 expenditures, including monthly and annual expenses (e.g., rent, groceries, insurance, giving). In the second column, estimate how much you spend or save for each category monthly. In the third column, write down the amount you believe aligns with God's best for your finances. Compare these figures to identify areas where your financial priorities could shift. Reflect on what surprised you, adjustments you could make, and actionable steps to better steward your resources in alignment with God's plan. Share what you discovered with someone.

Discipleship Practice

▸ **Financial Stewardship** | We recognize that financial resources are not ours to spend or manage but rather to steward. Therefore, we commit to making decisions about money with God's kingdom priorities in mind. *Why?* Being free from debt brings the joy of stewardship, which gives us the capacity to practice generosity.

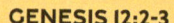

THE LORD SAID TO ABRAM, "I WILL BLESS YOU, AND ALL
PEOPLES ON EARTH WILL BE BLESSED THROUGH YOU."

GENESIS 12:2-3

God Blesses Abram to Bless the World

GENESIS 12:1-5

PURPOSE

1. To explore the beginning of God's long-term salvation plan.

2. To be willing to let go of what hinders us from immersing ourselves in God's worldwide mission.

DISCIPLESHIP THEME

Mission

PRAYER

Loving God, Father to all, ignite within us a passion to share your abundant blessings with the world. In this time, guide us. Reveal what we may need to let go of to become more active participants in your Kingdom's redemptive plan.

MEMORY VERSE

I will make you a great nation, and I will bless you and make your name great so that you will be a blessing. (Genesis 12:2)

DISCIPLESHIP PRACTICE

Short-Term, Cross-Cultural Experiences

Introduction

God created a perfect world, but sin and rebellion corrupted the life he intended in Eden. Even after events like the Flood and the Tower of Babel, God never abandoned humanity.

In Genesis 12:1-3, God, our Savior, and King, revealed the beginning of his plan to redeem humanity. This long-term plan started with a seemingly ordinary desert nomad named Abram (later called Abraham). God chose Abram's family as his special people and promised them land, descendants, and more.

The goal? For Abram's family to become a "blessing to all the nations" (Genesis 12:3). This meant leaving their familiar life and homeland to follow God's promises.

What was required of Abram and his family? They were to leave their clan, way of life, and the land where they had settled. God's plan centered on 1) his promise to bless Abram to be a blessing and 2) on Abram's willingness to trust God and leave everything.

Abram obeyed, and God kept his promises. Blessings flowed through Abram's descendants: Isaac, Jacob, and Joseph (Genesis 21-50). Despite their flaws, these patriarchs were the recipients of God's faithful promise-keeping.

This story marks the beginning (i.e., "genesis") of the Hebrew people. God's covenant with Abram establishes a pattern: He's always working to redeem the world.

Since Abraham, God has invited his followers to be his ambassadors. We are called to be "full-time ministers" of God's blessings, not just recipients. All of us, together and individually, are created to be involved in God's work of restoring his kingdom on earth (Matthew 6:10).

The characters in this story (Abram, Sarai, and their descendants) are not the heroes—their flaws make that clear. Similarly, our participation in God's mission is important, but its success ultimately depends on God. He is the hero from beginning to end. Our limitations do not keep God from using us in his mission.

The plan is simple: we are blessed to be a blessing. *But what does that truly mean for you, for me, and for us together?*

History shows that a plan's simplicity does not mean it will be well-executed. Abraham's descendants struggled to share God's blessings with others and surrounding nations. Jesus' disciples argued over who would be first. They wondered why the Master took time to talk to Samaritans and lepers and to bless little children.

What about the Church today?

Is more of its time, funding, and attention focused on being blessed ourselves than it is toward prioritizing the Kingdom of God?

Letting go of things we value can be a struggle. Abraham seemed to let go of his extended family and home easily. The Bible might not detail Abram's internal conflicts, but we can certainly imagine his challenges.

What might we need to let go of to fully serve as conduits of God's love, truth, and blessings to the world?

What Is Your Experience?

God wants the whole world to experience his generosity and blessings. He calls us to live a life marked by receiving and sharing God's abundance. However, our hearts and institutions often struggle with hoarding rather than sharing our blessings and abundance. Pick a starting group from the list:

- your peers
- your church or Christian group
- government or business leaders

Can you give a specific example of how this group or institution has misused or hoarded the resources entrusted to them?

_____

_____

_____

In what area(s) of your life do you find it challenging to be generous with the blessings God has given you?

_____

_____

_____

Explore the Story

Consider the Viewpoints | Genesis 12:1-5

Your group leader will assign you a character below. Notice what your character does and says, and then imagine their thoughts and feelings. Share some of your discussion highlights, any lingering questions, and how you can possibly relate to this character.

EVIL

Satan succeeded in introducing sin and its chaos into the world (Genesis 3-11). He would not be slow to do all he could to keep Abram from jump-starting God's redemption plan.

ISRAEL'S NEIGHBOR NATIONS

Many other nations or tribes surrounded Abram's family in the land of Canaan; many from all nations and tribes will one day surround the throne of the Lamb (Revelation 7:9). Throughout the larger story of the Bible, we know our missional God wants all nations in all generations to experience his blessings: "God so loved the world…" (John 3:16).

ABRAM AND SARAI

It does not seem that Abram or Sarai had any unique talents that made them God's obvious choice for his grand salvation plan. Abram was a leader of wandering nomads, and Sarai was an old, barren woman.

GOD THE HERO

Our restoring God revealed his plan to Abram to bring the world his healing and salvation. God was creating a rescuing people for himself that would one day find fulfillment in Jesus and the Church.

Lord God to Abram

"Go from your country, your people, and your father's household to the land I will show you. ² "I will make you into a great nation, and I will bless you; I will make your name great, and you will be a blessing. ³ I will bless those who bless you, and whoever curses you I will curse; and all peoples on earth will be blessed through you."

Narrator

⁴ So Abram went, as the Lord had told him, and Lot went with him. Abram was seventy-five years old when he set out from Harran. ⁵ He took his wife Sarai, his nephew Lot, all the possessions they had accumulated, and the people they had acquired in Harran, and they set out for the land of Canaan, and arrived there.

GENESIS 12:1-5

Comparing God's Call to Abraham to Jesus' Call to the First Disciples

Jesus' call to the first disciples (see Mark 1:16-18) shares several similarities with God's call to Abram (Genesis 12:1-5).

- ▶ Abram and the new disciples were given promises that involved them in a mission to lead, transform, and bless others.

- ▶ Both needed to leave precious things behind.

- ▶ Neither knew what lay ahead, yet they placed radical trust in the one calling them.

Live into the Story

God the Hero

Read the promises, blessings, and commands of Genesis 12:1-3 again. As you do, consider what they directly or indirectly reveal about the character of our missional God. Which of these descriptions stands out most to you? Fill in descriptions to complete this sentence:

In this story, God is _____

_____

_____

Our Story

What might Jesus' followers need to leave behind to be conduits of God's blessings and mission to the world? Pick 1 or 2 and explain.

- ▶ plans for our imagined and independent future

- ▶ our predictable routines and schedules

- ▶ our ability to live wherever with whatever possessions we want

- ▶ being in a comfortable and protected environment

- ▶ peer pressure and social expectations for how we should live

- ▶ other?

_____

_____

_____

_____

Which one of these from the list resonates with you the most? Please explain.

_____

_____

_____

_____

Reaching Others

God has blessed us to be a blessing to the world. What is one of God's specific blessings you can share with someone in your family, neighborhood, workplace, school, community, or the larger world?

_____

_____

_____

_____

Close Together in Prayer

Looking Ahead

Abram and Sarai respond in faith, leaving their homeland at God's command. Their journey sets the stage for the lives of their descendants—the patriarchs Isaac, Jacob, and Joseph—and their growing families. Over time, this family finds itself in Egypt and eventually at Mount Sinai, where they encounter a powerful and defining revelation from God.

Theory to Practice: *Response for Disciples*

Prayer Ideas

▸ Read Psalm 103:1-6. Take a moment afterwards to thank God for several of his specific blessings. Consider tangible things you can see and feel, like food, and a few intangible gifts, like peace.

▸ Choose one thing that's hindering you from being a blessing to others and take concrete action to overcome it.

▸ Pray for God's mission to be accomplished in a nation other than your own.

Action Ideas

▸ Commit to one action for someone you want to bless this week.

▸ Reflect on something you believe God might want you to leave behind. Offer this thing to God with an open heart. Then, ask for his empowering strength to help you release it.

▸ Explore the possibility of a cross-cultural trip or experience that is available this coming year.

Discipleship Practice

▸ **Cross-Cultural Experiences:** Individuals or groups are prepared for cross-cultural missions by being exposed to people, experiences, and realities of a different culture. *Why?* We need to build greater awareness and sensitivity to the larger world God loves and be ready to serve those from different cultures than our own.

GOD SPOKE THESE WORDS: "I AM THE LORD YOUR GOD WHO BROUGHT YOU OUT OF THE LAND OF EGYPT, YOU SHALL HAVE NO OTHER GODS BEFORE ME."

EXODUS 20:1-3

God Commands His People to Love

EXODUS 20:1-17

PURPOSE

1. To explore God's revelation on Mt. Sinai, where Israel is commanded in various ways to love the Lord and their neighbor.

2. To respond to God's love by promising to love God and the people he has put into our lives.

KINGDOM THEME

Promise-Making

PRAYER

God, open my eyes to see your enduring love and the truth within your commands. Empower my will to keep my commitments to love you and our neighbors.

MEMORY VERSE

Then God spoke these words: 'I am the Lord your God who brought you out of the land of Egypt, out of the house of slavery. You shall have no other gods before me.' (Exodus 20:1-3)

DISCIPLESHIP PRACTICE

Sabbath

Introduction

At the end of Genesis, we learn that God's people have been forced to settle in Egypt. Their initial favor wained and they were enslaved under a new Egyptian king. His Hebrew children cried out to God, toiling endless hours under the sun's blistering heat as slave drivers beat them into greater productivity.

What would God do now to continue the plan and promise he made to Abraham?

God raised Moses as his leader and used his power through Moses to bring miraculous plagues upon the land. Only then did Pharaoh finally release the Hebrews from Egypt.

Having proven that he was a more excellent king than Egypt's gods, Yahweh led the people through the Red Sea on dry land and then through the wilderness. He called Moses up to Mount Sinai and gave him the Commandments of his new covenant with Israel.

God's giving and our obeying of the Ten Commandments should be seen as part of a divine and dramatic love story. God intended his law to lead us into truth and life. In response, the Hebrew people were to promise they would be loyal, bound in heart, and willing to obey these commands.

As with the promises given to Abraham in Genesis 12:2-3, God intended this special relationship to extend beyond Israel's benefit. God blessed them with his covenant and truth to make them priests to the nations (Exodus 19:5).

God makes promises, and we are made in his image; making and keeping promises continues to be a central part of who we are. While our identity as God's children is centered in Christ alone, our enduring commitments in life's roles reveal and form who we are. Human character diminishes without promise-making. Our relationships suffer, and our communities cannot flourish.

The same God who made promises at Mount Sinai continues to keep those promises to his people. The One who offered commands to the Hebrews still speaks truth and invites us to make promises back to him and others.

What might happen in our world if we responded to God's initiation by making and keeping good promises?

What Is Your Experience?

In the book of Exodus, the Hebrews struggle to keep their commitments to God. They are certainly not alone in this. Read through the following statements. Mark the ones that best describe your struggles with keeping promises.

▸ I am easily distracted by things that happen to me in the moment.

▸ I give too much time to life-draining activities that are not God's best.

▸ I hate to miss out on what might come up in the moment, so I often avoid making commitments ahead of time to keep my options open.

▸ I have been disappointed by people who have not kept their promises to me. In return, I avoid commitments so that I am less likely to hurt or be hurt by others.

▸ I find it easy to avoid the responsibility that comes with commitments. I prefer my leisure, relaxing, and spontaneous time to hard work.

▸ I often over-commit myself and end up falling short of keeping my commitments; when that happens, I feel guilty.

▸ When I make a commitment, I want to keep it as perfectly as possible. This approach often consumes my attention and prevents me from seeing the needs of others.

Can you see anything in your personality or past life experiences that have led you to unhealthy ways of making and keeping commitments? Please explain.

_____

_____

_____

_____

_____

 # Explore the Story

Consider the Viewpoints | Exodus 20:1-17

Your group leader will assign you a character below. Notice what your character does and says, and then imagine their thoughts and feelings. Share some of your discussion highlights, any lingering questions, and how you can possibly relate to this character.

EVIL

Imagine Satan using two of his strategies at Mount Sinai to stop God's people from keeping their promises to God. The first would be to deemphasize God by turning his loving commands into mere rules, making obedience and trying harder the key to earning God's love. The second would be to forsake him for another idol.

OTHER NATIONS

As with Abraham, the divine revelations on Mt. Sinai started with Israel but were meant for all people. In Exodus 19:4-6, God called the Hebrew people to act like priests and to thoroughly pass on God's blessings to the nations. God intended Israel's obedience and witness to persuade the nations to also become his people.

THE HEBREW PEOPLE

In agreeing to the conditions of God's covenant, the formerly enslaved people were called to make promises to God and each other.

GOD

God revealed his greatness by freeing his people from slavery in Egypt. He then appeared to them with earthquakes and lightning on Mount Sinai. All this set the stage for his dramatic "wedding" covenant with his people, Israel.

Narrator

¹ And God spoke all these words:

Lord God

² "I am the Lord your God, who brought you out of Egypt, out of the land of slavery. ³ You shall have no other gods before me. ⁴ You shall not make for yourself an image in the form of anything in heaven above or on the earth beneath or in the waters below. ⁵ You shall not bow down to them or worship them; for I, the Lord your God, am a jealous God, punishing the children for the sin of the parents to the third and fourth generation of those who hate me, ⁶ but showing love to a thousand generations of those who love me and keep

(Scripture continues on the next page.)

my commandments. ⁷ You shall not misuse the name of the Lord your God, for the Lord will not hold anyone guiltless who misuses his name. ⁸ Remember the Sabbath day and keep it holy. ⁹ Six days you shall labor and shall do all your work, ¹⁰ but the seventh day is a sabbath to the Lord your God. On it you shall not do any work, neither you, your son or daughter, your male or female servant, your animals, or any foreigner residing in your towns. ¹¹ For in six days the Lord made the heavens and the earth, the sea, and all that is in them, but he rested on the seventh day. Therefore, the Lord blessed the Sabbath day and made it holy. ¹² Honor your father and your mother, so that you may live long in the land the Lord your God is giving you. ¹³ You shall not murder. ¹⁴ You shall not commit adultery. ¹⁵ You shall not steal. ¹⁶ You shall not give false testimony against your neighbor. ¹⁷ You shall not covet your neighbor's house. You shall not covet your neighbor's wife, or his male or female servant, his ox or donkey, or anything that belongs to your neighbor."

EXODUS 20:1-17

THE BIGGER STORY

Jesus' Summary of All God's Laws

Jesus summarized 613 Old Testament laws into just two: love God with all your heart, with all your soul, and with all your mind, and love your neighbor as yourself (Matthew 22:37-39). Notice how the first commands in Exodus 20 focus more on loving God and the last six on loving people. The simple focus of loving God and other people runs from the beginning to the end of the biblical story.

 # Live into the Story

God the Hero

List several attributes of God implied in Exodus 20:2.

_____

_____

Jesus' followers do not typically view the Ten Commandments as a means of better seeing God. Remember: commands by nature reveal something about the one who gives them. Pick two of the Exodus 20:3-17 commands that stood out to you most. Then ask what each command reveals about God's character (e.g., "do not lie" suggests God is honest and committed to the truth).

_____

_____

_____

_____

Our Story

Remember how you answered the **What Is Your Experience** question at the beginning of the lesson. How might your experience of this Exodus 20 lesson inspire you to now make and keep your commitments differently? Please explain.

_____

_____

_____

_____

Reaching Others

The people you want to love and serve were created to make and keep their commitments. They likely struggle with many of the same realities brought up in this lesson's **What Is Your Experience** question. What are several cultural expectations or forces that make it hard for people you serve to make and keep promises? Be specific.

_____

_____

_____

_____

Looking Ahead

After receiving the Levitical laws at Mount Sinai, the people of Israel regrouped and prepared to enter the land God had promised to their ancestors. They were positioned to move forward in obedience and take hold of God's blessings. However, a critical failure halted their progress. In our next lesson, we'll examine the story of the twelve spies—a turning point that reveals what kept God's people from entering the Promised Land and how fear, unbelief, and disobedience can derail the advancement of his Kingdom purposes.

Prayer Ideas

- Praise God for making and keeping all his promises from the Garden of Eden to today.

- Read Psalm 119:1-8. Thank God for his commands that allow you to follow him, show him your love and make promises of your own.

- Listen: Which one of the Exodus 20 commands might God want you to obey and say "yes" to in a fresh way? Ask God for help in obeying this command.

Action Ideas

- Identify one commitment you can make (or remake) and act on this week. Be clear about how and when you will act. Who can you share this with so they can pray for you this coming week?

- Designate 24 hours this week (e.g., all day Sunday or Saturday dinner to Sunday dinner) as your Sabbath. Identify the "work" activities you will not do and several refreshing activities you'll choose to experience alone or with others. Ideally, this will include your church service.

Discipleship Practice

- **Sabbath** | God designated one day each week to be set apart from the other six for rest and abstention from everyday work and consumer routines. This day is an opportunity to experience a little heaven on earth by engaging in activities that bring delight and renewal. *Why?* Because human nature tends to be covetous, we often take our responsibilities too seriously, and risk burning out and forgetting our dependence on God. We need a weekly chance to remember and be renewed in body, spirit, heart, mind, and will.

THEY SPREAD AMONG THE ISRAELITES A BAD REPORT ABOUT THE LAND THEY HAD
EXPLORED. THEY SAID, "THE LAND WE EXPLORED DEVOURS THOSE LIVING IN IT.
ALL THE PEOPLE WE SAW THERE WERE OF GREAT SIZE."

NUMBERS 13:32

Twelve Spies and Two Types of Fear

NUMBERS 13:25-14:11

PURPOSE

1. To understand the consequences of destructive fear in our lives and why God so often commands us not to be afraid.

2. To experience a faith that springs from a healthy "fear" of God, a faith that unleashes love and power that can overcome "giants."

KINGDOM THEME

Fear

PRAYER

God, I commit my time in this story to you. Please use this lesson to increase my faith and release me from fear's grip so that I may be free to engage well with you in life's challenges.

MEMORY VERSE

Only do not rebel against the Lord, and do not fear the people of the land, for they are no more than bread for us. Their protection is removed from them, and the Lord is with us. Do not fear them. (Numbers 14:9)

DISCIPLESHIP PRACTICE

Generosity

Introduction

On Mount Sinai, Israel's God Yahweh established a covenant relationship with his people. Soon after, he instituted sacrifices to deal with their ongoing acts of rebellion. God also promised to take his people to the Promised Land of Canaan, a journey of only forty days from Mount Sinai.

However, the book of Numbers ends decades later with them, not inside the Promised Land, but still outside on the edge.

What went wrong? Why didn't they enter right in?

Numbers 13:26-14:11 will help us see what happened.

God commanded Moses to send a group of twelve spies, one from each tribe, to survey the Promised Land. In our lesson's story, these spies returned with conflicting reports.

Ten of the spies focused mainly on the overwhelming might of the giants in the land. The other two spies were convinced that God would give them victory and that the Israelites should proceed with their plans.

Rather than face the giants and press forward, the people were gripped by fear. They yearned to go back to their predictable life of slavery in Egypt. Like all fear, the fear within the ten spies spread like fire. As a result, an entire generation was kept from entering the Promised Land.

We may ask ourselves, *how could they fear these giants when they'd seen God part the waters of the Red Sea and drown the pursuing Egyptian army?*

If we pause a moment, we can understand their fear. Fear of loss, disappointing others, being rejected, and fearing what will happen in the future grip the hearts of God's people, even though we should "know better."

Unhealthy fear pervades our personal and corporate lives—how we speak, how we think, what we decide to do, and how we decide do it. Stress and anxiety are often assumed to be unavoidable parts of our lives. It's too easy to accept our fears or learn to cope with them by hiding, self-medicating, or keeping busy. A play on words of a well-known biblical verse (1 John 4:18), it ends up that "perfect fear casts out love."

In contrast to the ten disbelieving spies, Joshua and Caleb exhibited a healthy fear—the fear of God.

Just what is the fear of the Lord?

It could be described as a combination of:

▸ a genuine reverence to God as holy King

▸ a healthy fear of disobedience's consequences

▸ taking God most seriously in all our decisions.

Yes, the fear of the Lord is the beginning of wisdom (Proverbs 1:7), the foundation of God's abundant life for us. It still remains an essential key to overcoming life's "giants" in today's chaotic world.

What Is Your Experience?

Name one big "fear-producing giant" (i.e., a personal situation or an issue your community, culture, or country) that causes you deep concern and stress. What negative consequence are you anticipating could happen?

_____

_____

_____

_____

What is one thing that this fear might be keeping you from experiencing in your relationships with God and/or other people? Please explain.

_____

_____

_____

_____

Explore the Story

Consider the Viewpoints | Numbers 13:26 - 14:11

Your group leader will assign you a character below. Notice what your character does and says, and then imagine their thoughts and feelings. Share some of your discussion highlights, any lingering questions, and how you can possibly relate to this character.

EVIL

Satan knows well the power that fear can have over people. Leaders in his grip can quickly spread fear in a community or culture, moving people away from practicing faith, hope, and love.

JOSHUA AND CALEB

These two men had long known each other and shared a common faith in God. They saw the same giants as the ten spies, so it seems fair to assume they would have faced their fears before they gave their positive report.

THE TEN SPIES

The report, which began by extolling the land's goodness and bounty, was followed by the word *'but'* (Numbers 13:28). The ten spies then gave a much longer report on the dangers presented by the giants.

GOD

God speaks only once in this story, yet we know he was always present. God grieves at his people's unbelief and unhealthy fear. Forty years of wandering in the wilderness, where he would continue to provide and be present, would be his "remedy."

Narrator

13:25 At the end of forty days they returned from exploring the land. 26 They came back to Moses and Aaron and the whole Israelite community at Kadesh in the Desert of Paran. There they reported to them and to the whole assembly and showed them the fruit of the land.

Ten Spies

27 "We went into the land to which you sent us, and it does flow with milk and honey! Here is its fruit. 28 But the people who live there are powerful, and the cities are fortified and very large. We even saw descendants of Anak there. 29 The Amalekites live in the Negev; the Hittites, Jebusites, and Amorites live in the hill country; and the Canaanites live near the sea and along the Jordan."

(Scripture continues on the next page.)

Narrator

³⁰ Then Caleb silenced the people before Moses and said,

Caleb

"We should go up and take possession of the land, for we can certainly do it."

Ten Spies

"We can't attack those people; they are stronger than we are."

Narrator

³² And the ten spies spread among the Israelites a bad report about the land they had explored.

Ten Spies

"The land we explored devours those living in it. All the people we saw there were of great size. ³³ We saw the Nephilim there. We seemed like grasshoppers in our own eyes, and we looked the same to them."

Narrator

¹⁴:¹ That night all the members of the community raised their voices and wept aloud.

Israelites

² "If only we had died in Egypt! Or in this wilderness! ³ Why is the Lord bringing us to this land only to let us fall by the sword? Our wives and children will be taken as plunder. Wouldn't it be better for us to go back to Egypt? We should choose a leader and go back to Egypt."

Narrator

⁵ Then Moses and Aaron fell face down in front of the whole Israelite assembly gathered there. ⁶ Joshua son of Nun and Caleb son of Jephunneh, who were among those who had explored the land, tore their clothes and said,

Joshua and Caleb

[7] *"The land we passed through and explored is exceedingly good.* [8] *If the Lord is pleased with us, he will lead us into that land, a land flowing with milk and honey, and will give it to us.* [9] *Only do not rebel against the Lord. And do not be afraid of the people of the land because we will devour them. Their protection is gone, but the Lord is with us. Do not be afraid of them."*

Narrator

[10] *But the whole assembly talked about stoning them. Then the glory of the Lord appeared at the tent of meeting all the Israelites.*

Lord God

[11] *"Moses, how long will these people treat me with contempt? How long will they refuse to believe in me despite all the signs I have performed among them?"*

NUMBERS 13:26 - 14:11

THE BIGGER STORY

Comparing the Twelve Spies and Jesus Walking on Water

In Matthew 14:22-32, Peter experienced the same confidence as Joshua and Caleb when he stepped out of the boat and walked toward Jesus standing on the sea. Peter looked down at the waves and was soon dominated by the same fear as the ten spies.

Perhaps we have all experienced both the unhealthy fear and the fear of God (or faith) in our hearts. Yet, like Peter, our divided hearts are welcomed into Jesus' fellowship and band of followers.

Live into the Story

God the Hero

The often-repeated command to "remember" is one of the Bible's most important. From this lesson's story, it's not hard to see why. List below several miracles God had performed for the Hebrews in Egypt and in the wilderness—miracles the ten spies had "forgotten."

_____

_____

_____

Now, list several character traits of God that these previous miracles made evident, i.e., character traits that the people should have remembered when they heard about the giants.

They forgot that God was...

_____

_____

_____

_____

Our Story

Remember the issue of fear you shared at the beginning of the lesson. The miracles *and* character traits of God, if we remember and hold them near, should free us from the paralyzing fear of our "giants."

Pick one of God's attributes from your list above you want to internalize. Then imagine and write down one practice that would help you remember God's character and his past deeds in your life. Be specific.

God attribute: _____

My "remember" practice: _____

Describe how this regular practice might help your faith in times of anxiety and fear.

_____

_____

_____

_____

Reaching Others

Social media, high expectations, prejudice, injustice, identity issues, economic uncertainty, political instability, and much more make anxiety almost impossible to avoid in our day. Think about a people group you feel called to serve. What are two main issues that cause them to fear, worry, and stress?

_____

_____

_____

In what specific way could you speak into their fear like Joshua or Caleb did in our story?

_____

_____

Close Together in Prayer

Looking Ahead

God declares his discipline for his rebellious people: They will wander in the wilderness for 40 years. During that time Moses dies and leadership passes to Joshua. Before Joshua's death, God—Israel's true King—leads his people into the Promised Land, fulfilling his promise. But their loyalty quickly fades. The book of Judges reveals how and why Israel spiraled into a cycle of unfaithfulness and struggle.

Prayer Ideas

- Talk to God about revealing any unhealthy fear and anxiety in your heart.

- Ask God for forgiveness, not for feeling fear but for allowing fear to make you forget his faithfulness in your life.

- Ask God for help to remember his past miracles and to move forward in the midst of "giants," convinced of God's victory.

Action Ideas

- Identify a specific practice to help you remember God's faithful works this week. Do this practice with someone you know who is gripped by fear and anxiety and who needs faith, like that of Joshua and Caleb.

- One of our fears is letting go of our financial resources. Identify a need that has been brought to your attention and make a financial contribution at a level that might make you feel uneasy.

Discipleship Practice

- **Generosity** - As God's stewards, we willingly love him and our neighbor by giving freely of our treasure, time and talents. *Why?* Because God has first extravagantly loved us, and we end up receiving more than we give.

THE PEOPLE OF ISRAEL SERVED THE BAALS AND THEY ABANDONED THE LORD,
WHO HAD BROUGHT THEM OUT OF THE LAND OF EGYPT.

JUDGES 2:11-12

Israel in Bondage to Idolatry

JUDGES 2:6-23

PURPOSE

1. To better appreciate our vulnerability to idols and the matching mercy of God toward those who worship them.

2. To identify cultural and personal temptations of idolatry.

KINGDOM THEME

Idolatry

PRAYER

Lord, help me better understand how idolatry enslaves. Use this lesson to help address this sin and temptation in my life. Renew my loyalty to your Son Jesus alone.

MEMORY VERSE

And the people of Israel did what was evil in the sight of the Lord and served the Baals and they abandoned the Lord, the God of their ancestors, who had brought them out of the land of Egypt. (Judges 2:11-12)

DISCIPLESHIP PRACTICE

Simplicity

Introduction

The book of Joshua closes with the twelve tribes living in the Promised Land; a large number of Canaan's inhabitants and idols remained there. These Canaanite deities created cancer-like cells that would soon poison Israel's loyalty to God.

Joshua's death opens the book of Judges. Israel still claimed God as their King but lacked a capable human leader to replace Joshua. Nevertheless, the Israelites attempted to complete their conquest of the Promised Land.

Instead of driving out the Canaanites as God had commanded, they forced many into slavery and allowed them to remain there. Because of this disobedience, God declared that Canaan's idols would become snares to Israel and the primary source of their ongoing spiritual downfall.

Generation after generation, the Israelites repeatedly forgot Yahweh's faithfulness and slid into their new neighbors' idolatry. Israel's initial worship of the gods Baal and Ashteroth involved erotic rituals with temple prostitutes—all these they practiced without shame. No matter their solemn promises, the twelve tribes could not love and worship God alone.

Just how did their idolatry bring on the people's demise?

Judges 2:6-23 outlines Israel's destructive cycle of sin. This cycle starts with Israel's current leader dying. When his people drift into idolatry and rebellion, the Lord is rightfully jealous and angry toward his wayward children. He faithfully pursues Israel by allowing her enemies to attack and encroach on her land. After the people are defeated, they cry out to God for rescue.

The Lord responds to their prayer by raising a Spirit-anointed military leader, a judge, who leads Israel to repel her enemies. Seeing God's hand of victory helps the people come to their senses and they rededicate their loyalty to God.

As long as the judge lived, the Israelites served God, experienced prosperity, and rested from war. When the judge dies, however, the people drift from gratitude and neglect their promises to stay loyal to God.

As a result, this cycle of sin repeats many times over the four centuries of the period of Judges. Israel needed their God's mercy and rescue.

Does idolatry still ravage the world and church?

A discerning eye can see idolatry present everywhere in the world. Anything or anyone that we offer an excessive amount of attention can masquerade as a god. Idols can be physical things such as beautiful homes, fancy cars, money, or delicious food. They can also be intangible things like work, relationships, happiness, or security.

Just like Israel in their worship of Baal, our false hope in idols leads us to bondage, addiction, and disappointment. Yet, this "cheating" on our loyalty to God does not move him to abandon us. His covenant jealousy, holy anger, and persistent rescue efforts all reveal our King's unrelenting love.

The Sin Cycle in Judges

This diagram summarizes the repeated elements of the Judges sin cycle described in the introduction. The cycle starts at the top with #1 and moves clockwise.

As you read this centuries-old cycle of Israel's sin, can you see any connections to your own country's cycle of sin and relationship to God?

On a personal note, which step(s) can you relate to most in your faith story?

_____

_____

_____

_____

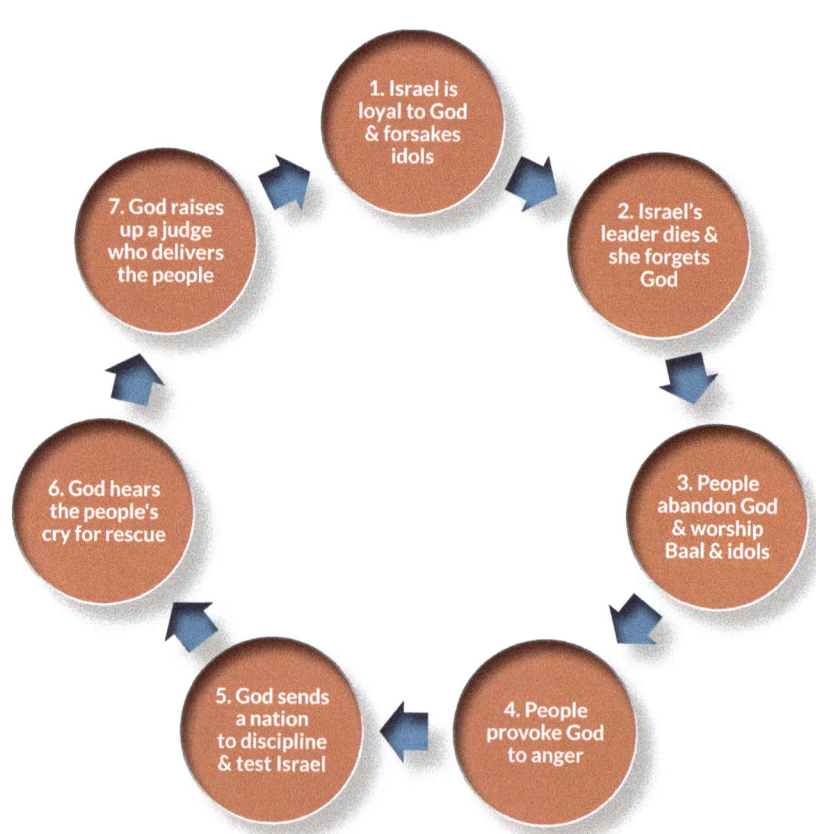

1. Israel is loyal to God & forsakes idols

2. Israel's leader dies & she forgets God

3. People abandon God & worship Baal & idols

4. People provoke God to anger

5. God sends a nation to discipline & test Israel

6. God hears the people's cry for rescue

7. God raises up a judge who delivers the people

What Is Your Experience?

Consider what your generation and peers devote more time, attention, passion, and money to other than God. In other words, what do they "worship"? Pick two of your culture's most popular or influential idols.

_____

_____

What invisible benefits do you or other people expect to receive from these two idols? Please explain.

_____

_____

_____

_____

Explore the Story

Consider the Viewpoints | Judges 2:6-23

Your group leader will assign you a character below. Notice what your character does and says, and then imagine their thoughts and feelings. Share some of your discussion highlights, any lingering questions, and how you can possibly relate to this character.

EVIL

It is one of the consistent strategies of the evil one to transform something or someone good or neutral into an idol. He would also tempt us to dilute our loyalty to God and then wrongly conclude that our divided heart matters not (Matthew 6:24).

THE JUDGES: ISRAEL'S LEADERS

God chose to raise up military leaders for his people in their times of crisis. After gaining victory over their oppressors, the judges temporarily became local administrators or national rulers, helping Israel revive their loyalty to God.

ISRAEL

The descendants of those who had witnessed God's mighty acts of deliverance drifted to disobedience. The twelve tribes who had pledged their loyalty to God became trapped in a cycle of idolatry.

GOD

The God who demanded to be central in the Garden of Eden rightly asked for worship without rivals. When the twelve tribes entered the Promised Land and fell prey to idolatry, God's persistent love toward Israel shone brightly.

Narrator

⁶ After Joshua had dismissed the Israelites, they went to take possession of the land, each to their own inheritance. ⁷ The people served the Lord throughout the lifetime of Joshua and of the elders who outlived him and who had seen all the great things the Lord had done for Israel. ⁸ Joshua, son of Nun, the servant of the Lord, died at the age of a hundred and ten. ⁹ And they buried him in the land of his inheritance, at Timnath Heres in the hill country of Ephraim, north of Mount Gaash. ¹⁰ After that whole generation had been gathered to their ancestors, another generation grew up who knew neither the Lord nor what he had done for Israel. ¹¹ Then the Israelites did evil in the eyes of the Lord and served the Baals. ¹² They forsook the Lord, the God of their ancestors, who had brought them out of Egypt. They followed and worshiped various gods of the people around them. They aroused the Lord's anger ¹³ because they forsook him and served Baal and the Ashtoreths. ¹⁴ In his anger against Israel the Lord gave them into the hands of raiders who plundered them. He sold them into the hands of their enemies all around, whom they were no longer able to resist. ¹⁵ Whenever Israel went out to fight, the hand of the Lord was against them to defeat them, just as he had sworn to them. They were in great distress. ¹⁶ Then the Lord raised up judges, who saved them out of the hands of these raiders. ¹⁷ Yet they would not listen to their judges but prostituted themselves to other gods and worshiped them. They quickly turned from the ways of their ancestors, who had been obedient to the Lord's commands. ¹⁸ Whenever the Lord raised up a judge for them, he was with the judge and saved them out of the hands of their enemies as long as the judge lived; for the Lord relented because of their groaning under those who oppressed and afflicted them. ¹⁹ But when the judge died, the people returned to ways even more corrupt than those of their ancestors, following other gods and serving and worshiping them. They refused to give up their evil practices and stubborn ways. ²⁰ Therefore the Lord was very angry with Israel and said

Lord God

"Because this nation has violated the covenant I ordained for their ancestors and has not listened to me, ²¹ I will no longer drive out before them any of the nations Joshua left when he died. ²² I will use them to test Israel and see whether they will keep the way of the Lord and walk in it as their ancestors did."

Narrator

²³ The Lord had allowed those nations to remain; he did not drive them out at once by giving them into the hands of Joshua.

JUDGES 2:6-23

| THE BIGGER STORY

Comparing Israel with the Prodigal Son

Notice some similarities between Israel's cycle of idolatry and the prodigal son's leaving and returning home to his father (Luke 15:11-24). Israel and the son rebelled and broke a relationship with their loving father. Both experience pain and deprivation. Both return and are welcomed back. God's love and mercy are as present in the Old Testament as they are in the New Testament.

Live into the Story

God the Hero

Write down words and images that summarize God's *actions* and *character* toward Israel in Judges 2.

_____

_____

_____

_____

Our Story

Knowing how God acted toward Israel in their bondage to idolatry, how might you approach Jesus the next time you find yourself caught in your cycle of sin, idolatry, or addiction? Be specific.

_____

_____

_____

_____

Reaching Others

Those offering Christ's freedom to others caught in idolatry's bondage should be familiar with how it often begins. How might someone's unchecked thoughts, desires, experiences, or expectations later lead to idolatry.

_____

_____

_____

_____

Looking Ahead

The book of Judges ends with a powerful summary of Israel's spiritual collapse: "In those days Israel had no king; everyone did what was right in his own eyes" (Judges 21:25). This moral chaos and social disorder sparked a growing desire for a human king—someone to lead them in battle and restore stability. In our next lesson, we'll explore how God, Israel's true King, responds to this longing by granting their request and appointing their first two human kings.

Theory to Practice: *Response for Disciples*

Prayer Ideas

‣ Thank God for his power and mercy, which can bring you freedom from your idolatry and addictions.

‣ Read Psalm 115:4-8. Confess to God a specific idol you struggle with. What next step is the Holy Spirit inviting you to do regarding your temptations with this idol?

Action Ideas

‣ Talk with a trusted friend or mentor to help identify one practical step you believe God wants you to take this week to find freedom from bondage to an idol.

‣ Identify which part of the Judges' sin cycle you can relate to most right now. Share this with someone.

‣ List several realities that might distract your passions, time, and attention from a simple and focused love of God. Write a short letter to God about these realities, and/or your need for help.

Discipleship Practice

‣ **Simplicity |** Stripping away the excesses that can clutter the heart and home nurtures contentment. Material simplicity involves living with less and prioritizing needs over wants. Heart simplicity is the practice of nurturing a jealous love for God and his Kingdom. *Why?* Simplicity guards the heart devotion of Jesus' followers and frees from the bondage of "muchness."

SAMUEL ASKED JESSE, "ARE THESE ALL YOUR SONS?" JESSE ANSWERED,
'THERE IS STILL THE YOUNGEST WHO IS TENDING THE SHEEP."
SAMUEL SAID, "SEND FOR HIM."

I SAMUEL 16:11

A King Is Chosen for Israel

1 SAMUEL 16:1-13

PURPOSE

1. To understand God's priority of the heart in David and all his leaders.

2. To embrace God's shaping of our hearts for our good and those we will serve.

MEMORY VERSE

But the Lord said to Samuel, 'Do not look on his appearance or on the height of his stature, because I have rejected him; for the Lord does not see as mortals see; they look on the outward appearance, but the Lord looks on the heart. (1 Samuel 16:7)

KINGDOM THEME

The Heart Journey

DISCIPLESHIP PRACTICE

Contemplative Prayer

PRAYER

God, send upon me the same Spirit you sent to anoint David. Fill my heart and deepen your work. Prepare me for what you have in store for my service to you and others.

Introduction

Recall the last sentence of the book of Judges: "In those days Israel had no king, but everyone did as they saw fit" (Judges 21:25). Out of their desire for peace and stability, Israel begged the prophet Samuel to appoint a flesh-and-blood king. They longed for a ruler whose voice they could hear, whose stature they could admire, and whose lead they could follow.

God granted their request despite his concern. He knew his people would drift from giving him his rightful place as king. Over the next several years, God led Samuel to anoint two kings, first Saul and then David.

Why were two kings appointed and not just one?

Although Saul was a tall, competent soldier, there is no record of any life circumstances that prepared his heart and character. We do know that the power of being king corrupted Saul's heart to rebel against God. What was true for Saul is true in our times as well: leadership responsibilities bring a new and powerful set of temptations.

On the other hand, David's heart was shaped by situations that tested and humbled him. His brothers looked down on him; in Eastern cultures age brings honor. Forced as the youngest to tend the family's sheep, David bore great responsibility but missed out on much of his family's respect and daily life.

God used David's experiences of wilderness isolation and danger to prepare his heart for future leadership over the kingdom of Israel. Solitude nurtured the practice of prayer. The humility he learned tending sheep later helped David readily admit his need for God's direction and strength.

After committing murder and adultery, David did not stray from God long. He would soon repent, turning back to loving and obeying his God.

No wonder God would later say David was a man after his own heart (1 Samuel 13:14, Acts 13:22).

Can you see how God's dealings with David might help reframe what we value in leaders and how we must be prepared before we try to influence others?

Instead of focusing first on our talents and potential impact, we should submit ourselves to God and a needed season of preparation.

Those who want to live into God's calling of leading their families, churches, businesses, classrooms, or organizations must start where God does: the cultivation of our hearts and character. As we let God deepen these foundations, we can be confident that the fruit of our labor will last.

What Is Your Experience?

Like Saul, those who take on leadership responsibilities will face a persistent and powerful set of temptations. Make a short list of temptations you believe leaders must be aware of and resist so they can remain effective servants of God.

_____

_____

_____

_____

Pick one of these temptations above that you can relate to or have experienced. Please explain.

_____

_____

_____

_____

 # Explore the Story

Consider the Viewpoints | 1 Samuel 16:1-13

Your group leader will assign you a character below. Notice what your character does and says, and then imagine their thoughts and feelings. Share some of your discussion highlights, any lingering questions, and how you can possibly relate to this character.

EVIL

The Enemy does not want God's leaders to be personally prepared or well-received by the people. He knows God's leadership plans will break down if he can corrupt the leader's heart or fortify the people's false expectations of a king.

DAVID

God used David's lower social standing to cultivate humility. He used isolation to refine David's heart and open his prayer life. Life as a shepherd taught David to rely entirely on God in this dangerous, tedious work.

SAMUEL

The dedicated boy who grew up serving Yahweh in the temple now carried the burden of leading the spiritually shallow nation of Israel. God asked Samuel to anoint a second king. Samuel arrived in Bethlehem, afraid of what Saul would do if he found out.

GOD

Israel's request for a human king undoubtedly troubled their holy and jealous Lord. God granted their request, but he grieved when Saul so quickly rebelled. The Lord was pleased to send Samuel to anoint David, an imperfect young man, but one "after God's own heart."

Lord God

[1] *"Samuel, how long will you mourn for Saul, since I have rejected him as king over Israel? Fill your horn with oil and be on your way; I am sending you to Jesse of Bethlehem. I have chosen one of his sons to be king."*

Samuel

[2] *"How can I go? If Saul hears about it, he will kill me."*

Lord God

"Take a heifer with you and say, 'I have come to sacrifice to the Lord.' [3] *Invite Jesse to the sacrifice, and I will show you what to do. You are to anoint for me the one I indicate."*

(Scripture continues on the next page)

Narrator

⁴ Samuel did what the Lord said. When he arrived at Bethlehem, the elders of the town trembled when they met him.

Elders

"Do you come in peace?"

Samuel

⁵ "Yes, in peace; I have come to sacrifice to the Lord. Consecrate yourselves and come to the sacrifice with me."

Narrator

Then he consecrated Jesse and his sons and invited them to the sacrifice. ⁶ When they arrived, Samuel saw Eliab and thought,

Samuel

"Surely the Lord's anointed stands here before the Lord."

Lord God

⁷ "Do not consider his appearance or his height, for I have rejected him. The Lord does not look at the things people look at. People look at the outward appearance, but the Lord looks at the heart."

Narrator

⁸ Then Jesse called Abinadab and had him pass in front of Samuel.

Samuel

"The Lord has not chosen this one either."

Narrator

⁹ Jesse then had Shammah pass by.

Samuel

"Nor has the Lord chosen this one."

Narrator

¹⁰ Jesse had seven of his sons pass before Samuel, but Samuel said to him,

Samuel

"The Lord has not chosen these. Are these all the sons you have?"

Jesse

"There is still the youngest, he is tending the sheep."

Samuel

"Send for him; we will not sit down until he arrives."

Narrator

¹² So he sent for him and had him brought in. He was glowing with health and had a fine appearance and handsome features.

Lord God

"Rise and anoint him; this is the one."

Narrator

¹³ So Samuel took the horn of oil and anointed him in the presence of his brothers, and from that day on, the Spirit of the Lord came powerfully upon David.

1 SAMUEL 16:1-13

THE BIGGER STORY

Jesus' Thirty Years of Preparation

Before being called the Messiah, Jesus also experienced a preparation period in his family and village life. God the Father used Jesus' first thirty "hidden" years in Nazareth to form his heart and character. For example, he learned to submit to authority under his parent's roof. Life with siblings taught him how to love and be unselfish. Jesus would have celebrated all the Jewish festivals, attended synagogue and studied and memorized the scriptures as a young Jewish boy. Jesus also developed his own relationship with God the Father.

Live into the Story

God the Hero

Consider God's words and actions in this story:

▶ *He commands Samuel to go on his behalf and anoint a new king.*

▶ *He declares his priority is the heart over outward appearance.*

▶ *He instructs Samuel on whom to choose and what to prioritize as a leader.*

▶ *He sends his Spirit to dwell on the shepherd boy David.*

What do these actions and words reveal about God's heart and character?

_____

_____

_____

_____

Our Story

God prepares the hearts of those he calls into his service. Share an example of God's work in your heart and character this past year or two.

_____

_____

_____

_____

Consider: How might this recent work of God in your heart and character prepare you to make a more significant "Jesus difference" in your family, workplace, church, or community? Be as specific as possible.

_____

_____

_____

_____

Reaching Others

Effective leadership requires being an inclusive communicator, empathetic listener, team player, willing delegator, servant to others, quality role model, courageous decision maker, and a bold activator. All these require both actions *and* heart realities. For example, to delegate well, leaders must have a heart free from the need to control, fear of failure, or need for constant attention and affirmation.

With this in mind, what is one specific thing a church or faith-based organization could do to prioritize a leader's heart in the process of leadership development? Be specific.

_____

_____

What might any workplace do to prioritize a leader's heart and character development?

_____

_____

Close Together in Prayer

Looking Ahead

In this lesson, we saw that God desires leaders whose hearts reflect his own—loving, compassionate, humble, and committed to righteousness. Yet the kings who followed David consistently fell short. Their failure in moral and spiritual leadership led the people to quickly abandon their covenant of faithfulness. In response, God raised up prophets—new agents of his salvation—who spoke his warnings to both leaders and common people. The first major figure in this prophetic role was Elijah.

Prayer Ideas

▸ Praise God for his own dear heart and Jesus' example of a long season of preparation. Ask the Lord to help you see your heart as he does.

▸ Read Psalm 139:23-24. Find a quiet and peaceful space or imagine one. Believe Christ is present with you. Breathe in the "air" of his love and exhale any fear or shame. Let your heart and thoughts rest in the arms of God's love.

Action Ideas

▸ Invite a friend to help you identify one "I need to grow" area of your life that would better prepare you to influence others. Identify several steps toward growing in that area.

▸ Write a short letter from God to you or from you to God concerning one of the following questions:

How has God has already prepared your heart to be a leader?

How might God right now be changing your heart and preparing you to be a more significant influence in the world?

Share the letter with someone who knows you well and ask for their response.

Discipleship Practice

▸ **Contemplative Prayer** | Prayer that moves from the mind being most active to being receptive to the more intimate experience of God's love and presence. *Why?* To increase our capacity for love and justice with God, our neighbor, and our messy, polarized world.

THE FIRE OF THE LORD
FELL AND BURNED UP
THE SACRIFICE, THE WOOD,
THE STONES, AND THE SOIL,
AND ALSO LICKED UP
THE WATER IN THE TRENCH.

1 KINGS 18:38

Elijah Brings the Fire of God

1 KINGS 18:17-42

PURPOSE

1. To understand the mission of Old Testament prophets—God's messengers urging his people to abandon evil and return to him.

2. Let Elijah's prayer inspire us to be intercessors—speaking to God on behalf of others and speaking to others on behalf of God.

MEMORY VERSE

Elijah said, 'How long will you go limping about with two different opinions? If the Lord is God, follow Him. And if Baal, follow Him.' (1 Kings 18:21)

DISCIPLESHIP THEME

Intercession

DISCIPLESHIP PRACTICE

Intercessory Prayer

PRAYER

Lord, may your Spirit's fire make Elijah's story alive to me. Teach me through his example to speak your words to others. Prepare me to speak to you on behalf of others and to pray for our own small miracles.

Introduction

After David's reign ended, Israel's new kings led the people back into an evil pattern of idolatry. The comforts of kingly prosperity infected David's son, Solomon, who enslaved his people to build an increasingly opulent palace. His heavy-handed demands led to deep and lasting discontentment among his subjects. As a result, the initially united kingdom split upon Solomon's death.

After the split, the ten northern tribes were called Israel and followed a new king. The other two tribes in the south became Judah. Under the following generations of evil kings, the priests again encouraged the people to worship Baal alongside Yahweh.

Moral recklessness became rampant among people ignorant of God's laws and ways.

How would the Lord come to their rescue this time?

In addition to previous salvation strategies of raising priests, judges, and kings, Yahweh now raised up a new kind of leader: the prophet. Elijah launched a several-century season in which God sent prophets to speak his truth to his people.

God pronounced through Elijah a judgment of drought upon an idolatrous Israel and her leaders, King Ahab and Queen Jezebel. After several years, God called on Elijah to end the drought.

This was followed by Elijah's challenge for a bold duel between Yahweh and Baal. God intended this dramatic miracle to compel Israel to repent and renew her loyalty to God alone.

The compelling story of Elijah in 1 Kings 18 gives us a timely opportunity to consider the role of prophets in the life of God's people.

These spokespeople for God urged Israel and her corrupt leaders to repent of oppressing the weak and lulling the people into idolatry.

However, the leaders and people of Israel often refused to listen to the prophets' warnings and exhortations. Kings even killed prophets to eliminate their persistent disruption of the evil status quo.

Prophets not only spoke to people on behalf of God but also to God on behalf of the people. These two sides of intercession still hold true today. Elijah's prayer to Yahweh in the climactic scene of 1 Kings 18

reveals the power and priority of intercessory prayer, as God alone brings fire from heaven— turning hearts and changing lives.

The era of prophetic ministry continued long after the Old Testament. Jesus, in his earthly preaching and prayers, was a prophet and intercessor like none other.

Are prophets still part of God's kingdom plan today?

Called to be like Jesus, some disciples are gifted by God to the ministry of intercession and prophecy (Ephesians 4:11, 1 Corinthians 14:1-5). There is still a need for timely words of exhortation and for praying to God on behalf of others.

Imagine what would happen if Jesus followers in every church followed Elijah's and Jesus' two-steps of praying for others and proclaiming God's truth with boldness.

What Is Your Experience?

The prophets sent in the Old Testament challenged God's people to turn from their sinful ways and renew their loyalty to God alone. Consider together: How are God's people in your culture tempted to water down their loyalty to Jesus? List several and be as specific as you can.

_____

_____

_____

_____

# Explore the Story

Consider the Viewpoints | 1 Kings 18:17-42

Your group leader will assign you a character below. Notice what your character does and says, and then imagine their thoughts and feelings. Share some of your discussion highlights, any lingering questions, and how you can possibly relate to this character.

EVIL

If the Enemy cannot make us renounce our devotion to God, he will tempt us to mix our "loyalty" to God with something or someone else. God's fire from heaven might lead Israel to move away from their idolatry; the Enemy surely doesn't want that to happen!

THE PEOPLE OF ISRAEL

The people in today's story either watch, remain silent, or respond briefly. Elijah hopes they will move from their passivity to a renewed zeal for following their God alone.

ELIJAH

Elijah was God's prophet, intercessor, and ambassador. Hiding in the wilderness during the famine prepared him for Mount Carmel's glorious duel and miracle.

GOD

God pursued his people with long suffering both by bringing famine to the land and by raising up the prophet Elijah for a dramatic and divine display of power.

Ahab

[17] "Is that you, you troubler of Israel?"

Elijah

[18] "I have not made trouble for Israel, but you and your father's family have. You have abandoned the Lord's commands and have followed the Baals. [19] Now summon the people from all over Israel to meet me on Mount Carmel. And bring the four hundred and fifty prophets of Baal and the four hundred prophets of Asherah, who eat at Jezebel's table."

Narrator

[20] So Ahab sent word throughout all Israel and assembled the prophets on Mount Carmel.

(Scripture continues on the next page)

Elijah

[21] "How long will you waver between two opinions? If the Lord is God, follow him; but if Baal is God, follow him."

Narrator

But the people said nothing.

Elijah

[22] "I am the only one of the Lord's prophets left, but Baal has four hundred and fifty prophets. [23] Get two bulls for us. Let Baal's prophets choose one for themselves and let them cut it into pieces and put it on the wood but not set fire to it. I will prepare the other bull and put it on the wood but not set fire to it. [24] Then you call on the name of your god, and I will call on the name of the Lord. The god who answers by fire—he is God."

People

"What you say is good."

Elijah to Prophets of Baal

[25] "Choose one of the bulls and prepare it first since there are so many of you. Call on the name of your god, but do not light the fire."

Narrator

[26] So they took the bull given to them and prepared it. Then they called on the name of Baal from morning till noon.

Baal Prophets

"Baal, answer us!"

Narrator

But there was no response; no one answered. And they danced around the altar they had made.
[27] At noon, Elijah began to taunt them.

Elijah

"Shout louder! Surely he is a god! Perhaps he is deep in thought, or busy[1], or traveling. Maybe he is sleeping and must be awakened."

Narrator

[28] So they shouted louder and slashed themselves with swords and spears, as was their custom, until their blood flowed. [29] Midday passed, and they continued their frantic prophesying until the time for the evening sacrifice. But there was no response; no one answered, and no one paid attention.

Elijah to the People

[30] "Come here to me."

Narrator

The people came to him, and he repaired the altar of the Lord, which had been torn down. [31] Elijah took twelve stones, one for each of the tribes descended from Jacob, to whom the word of the Lord had come, saying, "Your name shall be Israel." [32] With the stones he built an altar in the name of the Lord, and he dug a trench around it large enough to hold two seahs[2] of seed. [33] He arranged the wood, cut the bull into pieces, and laid it on the wood.

Elijah

[34] "Fill four large jars with water and pour it on the offering and on the wood. Do it again... Do it a third time."

Narrator

[35] The water ran down around the altar and even filled the trench. [36] At the time of sacrifice, the prophet Elijah stepped forward and prayed:

Elijah

"Lord, the God of Abraham, Isaac, and Israel, let it be known today that you are God in Israel and that I am your servant and have done all these things at your command. [37] Answer me, Lord, so these people will know that you, Lord, are God and that you are turning their hearts back again."

---

1   The literal meaning here is "relieving himself."

2   About 3 gallons.

Narrator

38 Then the fire of the Lord fell and burned up the sacrifice, the wood, the stones, and the soil, and also licked up the water in the trench. 39 When all the people saw this, they fell prostrate and cried,

People

"The Lord—he is God! The Lord—he is God!"

Elijah

40 "Seize the prophets of Baal. Don't let anyone get away!"

Narrator

They seized them and Elijah had them brought down to the Kishon Valley and slaughtered them there.

Elijah to Ahab

41 "Go, eat and drink, for there is the sound of a heavy rain."

Narrator

42 So Ahab went off to eat and drink, but Elijah climbed to the top of Carmel, bent down to the ground, and put his face between his knees.

1 KINGS 18:17-42

THE BIGGER STORY

Examples of Intercessory Prayers

Elijah's prayer (vv. 36-37) is only one of many intercessory prayers in the Bible. See also:

- ▶ Abraham's prayer in Genesis 18:16-33
- ▶ Moses' prayer in Exodus 32:1-14
- ▶ Nehemiah's prayer in Nehemiah 1:4-11
- ▶ Daniel's prayer in Daniel 9:3-19
- ▶ Jesus' prayer in John 17
- ▶ Paul's prayer in Ephesians 3:14-19

Live into the Story

God the Hero

What words would you use to summarize what God was like in this story?

_____

_____

For comparison, describe what Baal was like in this story and note the difference.

_____

_____

_____

Our Story

What could make the regular practice of intercessory prayer difficult for Jesus' followers? Circle one or more of the personal and cultural struggles below that most make consistent intercessory prayer hard for you.

- ▶ Busyness

- ▶ Taking what we do more seriously than what God does

- ▶ Lack of compassion

- ▶ Self-centeredness

- ▶ Lack of role models or experience with prayer of any kind

- ▶ Laziness

- ▶ Misperceptions about prayer

- ▶ Uncertainty that God would hear and answer us

Please explain your choices.

_____

_____

_____

_____

_____

Reaching Others

Imagine God is calling you to intercede between him and his people. Pick one of the issues you identified in the **What is Your Experience** question. Then, revisit Elijah's prayer in vv. 36-37 to look for valuable ideas and themes. Now, rewrite Elijah's short prayer into your own words to help you pray on behalf of your church or group regarding this issue.

_____

_____

_____

_____

_____

Close Together in Prayer

Looking Ahead

The people's loyalty to God was brief. They quickly returned to idolatry, adding the oppression of the poor to their sins. Meanwhile, the corruption of Israel's kings worsened. In response, God raised up new prophets to warn the people and deliver His loving discipline and judgment. However, for nearly 200 years, few heeded these warnings. As promised, God eventually brought his discipline upon Israel. The Babylonian army destroyed Jerusalem, and many Hebrews were taken into exile. From Jerusalem, the prophet Jeremiah later sent a letter to the exiles, offering them a difficult but hopeful message from the Lord.

Theory to Practice: *Response for Disciples*

Prayer Ideas

- Pray to God on behalf of your church or group, ideally starting with the short prayer written from the **Reaching Others** exercise above.

- Read Psalm 122:6-9, replacing Jerusalem with your country. Pray this prayer, modifying any of the words as needed. Briefly intercede on behalf of your country.

- Choose a difficult person or situation to pray for. Remember that Elijah prayed many times for months before the rain came down.

Action Ideas

- Share your prayer from the **Reaching Others** exercise on the previous page with someone. Share how it fits into the 1 Kings 18 Elijah story. Ask for their response.

- Rewrite the lesson's 1 Kings 18 story to fit your 21st century setting. Share it with someone and ask for their response.

- Go online and search for the history of revival in the world or in your country. What was something important you learned?

Discipleship Practice

- **Intercessory Prayer** | One or more people, with the Spirit's help, asking God to intervene on behalf of another person, group, issue and/or nation. *Why is this important?* As those now sitting with Christ at God's right hand, we are privileged to pray on behalf of others with God's authority, favor and promises.

PRAY TO THE LORD FOR THE CITY TO WHICH I HAVE CARRIED YOU,
BECAUSE IF YOU SEEK ITS SHALOM, YOU TOO WILL FIND YOUR SHALOM.

JEREMIAH 29:7

Jeremiah Brings God's Hope to Babylon

JEREMIAH 29:1-14

PURPOSE

1. To understand that God's surprising plans and hope for his people include the transformation of cities and communities.

2. To commit to working and praying toward transformation in your community.

MEMORY VERSE

Seek the shalom of the city where I have sent you into exile, and pray to the LORD on its behalf, for in its shalom you will find your shalom. (Jeremiah 29:7)

KINGDOM THEME

Shalom in the City

DISCIPLESHIP PRACTICE

Lament

PRAYER

God, forgive me for any ways I have made the 'plans I have for you' (Jeremiah 29:11) only for my well-being and not including the people and place where I live. Reveal to me your plans for how your people can seek the well-being of our community.

Introduction

The high point of Israel's early history was David's reign and Solomon's temple-building. However, this nation experienced persistent immorality and mutiny, eventually causing the split of the northern and southern kingdoms. Both Israel and Judah spiraled downward as they followed leaders who did not follow the Lord.

God raised up messengers called prophets who were sent with a divine message: "Repent from your ruts of rebellion, from your idolatry and oppression of the poor. Return to your God and your covenant with him. If you do, he will have mercy and pardon you. If you do not, you will experience sin's judgment and discipline."

One of those prophets was Jeremiah. He began his ministry during the reign of Judah's last good king, Josiah. This righteous leader listened to the prophets and grieved his people's perpetual unfaithfulness. He set the nation of Israel back on a course of worshiping the one true God.

However, the people only followed Josiah's reforms for a short time. Like their forefathers, they failed to trust in God alone and once again worshiped foreign gods.

Like the prophets before him, Jeremiah first delivered a strong warning for their continual disobedience. No surprise: the people ignored him.

They preferred to listen to the seductive promises of the false prophets.

After Josiah died in 609 BC, God's predictions came true. The second Babylonian empire flexed its military muscles by invading Judah in 607 BC and conquering all of Judah except for Jerusalem.

Nebuchadnezzar's army launched a second siege on Jerusalem in 597 BC and a final siege in 586. The campaign ended with the destruction of Jerusalem and its temple. Judah's most prominent citizens were deported: professionals, priests, judges, artisans, officials, and the wealthy. God demolished both Jerusalem and Judah's belief that Baal was the source of their well-being.

After the Babylonians destroyed Jerusalem, how did Jeremiah's message change?

Jeremiah began to offer God's hope and consolation to encourage the Jews' faith. He proclaimed a new work of God that would rebuild and prosper his people. Hebrew prophets often repeated this pattern of bringing words of hope after warnings of judgment. This lesson will focus on those words of hope to the Jewish exiles living in Babylon.

The commands and promises of Jeremiah 29 revealed God's heart and hope for his people in Babylon: to plant roots and seek their "enemy's"

salvation. If they did so, Yahweh's discipline would transform them. They would offer Babylon a compelling witness of his kingdom.

God also promised the exiles that they would return to Jerusalem after seventy years. Those hearing these promises would all be dead. Nevertheless, God's future hope greatly affected their present days in Babylon.

Seventy years later, Jeremiah's words came true. King Cyrus conquered Babylon and granted the exiles permission to return home.

Like the Jews of the 6th century BC, followers of Jesus today also live as exiles. Many today do not welcome the perspective of Christian faith into the public conversation. We need to hear again God's surprising plans for our future.

As for the exiles in Babylon, seeking God involves loving people we might not naturally choose and living in places we might prefer to avoid. Jesus' followers are still sent by God into challenging environments to provide a model of hope and wholeness.

Jeremiah 29 has lasting significance for Jesus' followers who are asking the question, "*What are God's plans for us living in today's 'Babylon'?*"

What Is Your Experience?

God intended to send the Jewish exiles to the city of Babylon to experience and model his goodness there. Identify a group of people in your community who experience hardship and hopelessness or a group where God could send you and his people to bring his flourishing.

_____

_____

Imagine one thing your church could do to help bring God's hope to this group.

_____

_____

Explore the Story

Consider the Viewpoints | Jeremiah 29:1-14

Your group leader will assign you a character below. Notice what your character does and says, and then imagine their thoughts and feelings. Share some of your discussion highlights, any lingering questions, and how you can possibly relate to this character.

EVIL

Babylon intended to grind the exiled Hebrews' patriotism into dust, to abolish once and for all God's redemption plan for the world. The false prophets, servants of the evil one, promised that exile in Babylon would last only two years before they returned to Jerusalem (Jeremiah 28:1-4).

THE PEOPLE OF BABYLON

Exiles from many conquered lands filled Babylon's streets. A collage of slaves, merchants, wise men, officials, laborers, harlots, and worshipers of many different gods dwelt there. Moral laxity, pride, oppression, and pleasure-seeking dominated the atmosphere.

JEWISH PARENTS IN EXILE

Those exiled from the ruined Jerusalem hated being transplanted in the land of their enemies, but they ended up raising their children in Babylon. As with immigrant families today, the experience of the first generation differed significantly from that of the second.

GOD

The God who created, called, and patiently pursued Israel over the centuries did not abandon the exiles in Babylon. God would surprise his people with promises of overwhelming abundance and wholeness for his people and the nations.

Narrator

¹ This is the text of the letter that the prophet Jeremiah sent from Jerusalem to the surviving elders among the exiles and to the priests, the prophets, and all the other people Nebuchadnezzar had carried into exile from Jerusalem to Babylon. ² This was after King Jehoiachin and the queen mother, the court officials and the leaders of Judah and Jerusalem, the skilled workers and the artisans had gone into exile from Jerusalem. ³ He entrusted the letter to Elasah son of Shaphan and to Gemariah, son of Hilkiah, whom Zedekiah king of Judah carried to King Nebuchadnezzar in Babylon. ⁴ It said:

This is what the Lord Almighty, the God of Israel, says to all those I sent into exile from Jerusalem to Babylon.

(Scripture continues on the next page.)

The Lord

⁵ "Build houses and settle down; plant gardens and eat what they produce. ⁶ Marry and have sons and daughters; find wives for your sons and give your daughters in marriage, so they too may have sons and daughters. Increase in number there; do not decrease. ⁷ Also, seek the peace and prosperity of the city to which I have carried you into exile. Pray to the Lord for it, because if it prospers, you too will prosper.

⁸ Do not let the prophets and diviners among you deceive you. Do not listen to the dreams you encourage them to have. ⁹ They are prophesying lies to you in my name. I have not sent them.

¹⁰ When seventy years are completed for Babylon, I will come to you and fulfill my good promise to bring you back to this place. ¹¹ For I know the plans I have for you, plans to prosper you and not to harm you, plans to give you hope and a future. ¹² Then you will call on me and come and pray to me, and I will listen to you. ¹³ You will seek me and find me when you seek me with all your heart. ¹⁴ I will be found by you, and will bring you back from captivity. I will gather you from all the nations and places where I have sent you, and will bring you back to the place from which I carried you into exile."

JEREMIAH 29:1-14

| **THE BIGGER STORY**

Jesus Also Commanded Us to Love Our "Enemies"

Jesus' command for his followers to love and pray for their enemies (Matthew 5:43-48) was not new; the exiles were commanded to do the same in Babylon (Jeremiah 29:6-7). But how many of those exiles abandoned their resentment toward their "enemies" and sought Babylon's good (Psalm 137:8-9, e.g.)? Not many. They, like us, needed Jesus' model of how to love our city and pray for our enemies.

 **Live into the Story**

God the Hero

Read below the summary of God's commands and promises given to the Jews in Babylon in Jeremiah 29. Then, answer the final two questions.

God's Commands

Build houses and settle down; plant gardens and eat what they produce.

Marry and have sons and daughters; find wives for your sons and give your daughters in marriage. Increase in number there; do not decrease.

Seek and pray for the shalom of the city to which I have carried you into exile.

Do not let the prophets and diviners among you deceive you. Do not listen to the dreams you encourage them to have.

Call on me and come and pray to me; seek me with all your heart.

God's Promises

In Babylon's shalom you will find your shalom.

When seventy years are completed for Babylon, I will gather you from all the nations and places where I have banished you; I will bring you back from captivity to the place from which I carried you into exile.

I will listen to you. You will seek me and find me. I will be found by you.

What do these commands and promises imply about

a) God's character:

_____

_____

_____

b) the kind of relationship God wants to have with people in "Babylon":

_____

_____

_____

Our Story

Review the Jeremiah 29 commands and promises in the **God the Hero** section. Summarize in your own modern words the present and future "plans" God has for us.

_____

_____

_____

_____

Reaching Others

In the short or long run, what people group would you like to be more involved with in bringing God's shalom and restoration to your community? Please elaborate.

_____

_____

_____

_____

Close Together in Prayer

Looking Ahead

Jeremiah's prophecy gave the first generation of Hebrew exiles in Babylon hope for a future return to Jerusalem. Figures like Daniel, Shadrach, Meshach, and Abednego held onto this promise, serving faithfully in Babylon's government. Decades later, Nehemiah, a descendant of these exiles, rose to a key leadership role under the Persian king and led Jerusalem's people in rebuilding their city. Nehemiah's leadership, rooted in faith and prayer, offers a powerful example of what it takes to guide broken communities toward restoration and flourishing.

Theory to Practice: *Response for Disciples*

Prayer Ideas

▸ Read Psalm 35:4-6 as one example of how people in the Old Testament prayed regarding their enemies. Thank Jesus for his love and prayer toward his executioners: "Father, forgive them, for they don't know what they are doing."

▸ Identify and pray for several of your community's leaders, institutions, and challenging situations.

▸ Open up your Bible to Psalm 13, an ancient prayer of lament. As you read, consider how someone experiencing loss or pain today might relate to some of its verses. As you read this lament a 2nd time, pray it as if you are experiencing loss or pain.

Action Ideas

▸ Listen to God for a small contribution you can make to God's plans for flourishing (i.e., shalom) in your community. Commit to do what God has placed on your heart.

Possible ideas: Consider encouraging a store clerk, helping someone in their yard or garden, inviting a friend to do a prayer walk in the city, or writing a thank-you letter to someone who serves you.

Discipleship Practice

▸ **Lament |** When our difficulties overwhelm us, we can bring them honestly before God with full sadness and declare our trust that he is still in control and hears our cries. *Why is this important?* The Psalms tutor us to pray this way, grounding us in God and his hope when we might otherwise despair.

THE WORK IS EXTENSIVE AND WE ARE WIDELY SEPARATED. WHEREVER YOU HEAR THE SOUND OF THE SHOFAR, JOIN US THERE. OUR GOD WILL FIGHT FOR US!

NEHEMIAH 4:19-20

The Rebuilding of Jerusalem's Walls

SELECTIONS FROM NEHEMIAH 1-4

PURPOSE

1. To understand how Nehemiah's leadership cultivated God's shalom and purposes.

2. To explore ways God can use and empower people today to lead like Nehemiah.

MEMORY VERSE

You see the trouble we are in, how Jerusalem lies in ruins with its gates are burned. Come, let us rebuild the wall of Jerusalem, so that we may no longer suffer disgrace. (Nehemiah 2:17)

DISCIPLESHIP THEME

Leadership

DISCIPLESHIP PRACTICE

Leadership

PRAYER

God, thank you for your heart to transform our cities and communities and sending your Son Jesus as the perfect Leader. Spirit, use Nehemiah's example to open my eyes to a deeper appreciation of transforming leadership in our day.

Introduction

Jeremiah's prophecy inspired the first generation of Hebrew exiles in Babylon to look forward to a better future, the day when God would fulfill his promise and allow their descendants to return to Jerusalem. At least a few of them, such as Daniel, Shadrach, Meshach, and Abednego, believed his message. These four served in the city's government with integrity and without compromise.

Just as God's prophet Jeremiah had predicted, the Persian ruler Cyrus II conquered the Babylonians seventy years after the first wave of exiles had left Jerusalem (Jeremiah 29:10). His royal edict allowed the Jewish exiles to return home. Most, however, chose to remain in Babylon in their new "home." Those who did return saw their beloved but broken-walled city for the first time.

Years later, a new Persian king, Artaxerxes, ruled over the Babylon region and chose Nehemiah as his cupbearer. God used this role to equip him with the character and skills necessary to mobilize the Jerusalem inhabitants into action.

Here are some leadership practices that made Nehemiah a successful leader: a vibrant prayer life, an observant eye, a willingness to delegate, an ability to motivate, tenacity and tact with both enemies and head rulers, and unrelenting faith in

Israel's God. All these prepared Nehemiah well to lead Jerusalem's discouraged people to rebuild her city's walls first and then their way of life.

Our reflection on Nehemiah's example must start when he still lived in Babylon. Nehemiah listened well to messengers who had just come from Jerusalem and reported on its broken walls and people. Nehemiah mourned, lamented, and confessed to God the sins of his people and included himself—even though he "wasn't there."

Upon these faith foundations would lay the success of Nehemiah's leadership back in Jerusalem.

What can leaders today learn from Nehemiah?

Here's one way to describe leadership: the ability to influence a group of people toward a challenging goal through motivating, modeling, mobilizing and mentoring. Leaders are needed to move people closer to a shared good for all toward God's shalom, i.e., his original design of flourishing, wholeness, and restoration. However, leaders in many civic institutions and community organizations often pursue self-serving interests. It is not human nature for leaders to act primarily as stewards of God's resources and servants of the people.

Power's twin is self-seeking. Corruption and greed easily overpowers servanthood. Good leaders are easy to follow but hard to find.

Our modern cities are filled with broken social systems and broken-hearted people. Walls of all kinds need God's repair; however, all is not lost. Our Lord and King is ready and always present with the power and desire to transform neighborhoods, organizations, and communities.

The book of Nehemiah provides a solid look into the life of a God-centered leader. It reminds us of the crucial role leaders must play if our communities are to change and flourish.

What Is Your Experience?

List several physical, relational, social, or economic needs (i.e., "crumbling walls") that you believe today's leaders should be helping repair either in our community or our country.

_____

_____

_____

Next, list several skills and character traits you think leaders should possess to serve people best, help people repair "walls," and facilitate lasting change in communities. Such leaders could include a teacher, principal, coach, pastor, administrator, boss, politician, parent, etc.

_____

_____

_____

Explore the Story

Consider the Viewpoints | Selections from Nehemiah 1-4

Your group leader will assign you a character below. Notice what your character does and says, and then imagine their thoughts and feelings. Share some of your discussion highlights, any lingering questions, and how you can possibly relate to this character.

EVIL

The Enemy uses humans outside of us and forces inside of us to frustrate our efforts to accomplish God's will. Leaders must be aware of the opposition they will personally face in their God-initiated efforts.

THE PEOPLE LIVING IN JERUSALEM

The people living in Jerusalem were a mix: the peasants left at the Babylonian exile and those who had decided to return after 537 BC. No attempt had been made to rebuild their city's walls and gates. And without city walls, their surrounding enemies invaded and plundered at will. They needed a leader.

NEHEMIAH

As the Persian king's trusted cupbearer, Nehemiah possessed a trustworthy character, but also leadership skills, charisma, natural talent and faith in God.

GOD

God does not speak directly in our story but Nehemiah often speaks to God. Though not mentioned, God remained present from the beginning to the end of the rebuilding of Jerusalem's walls.

Messengers from Jerusalem Speak to Nehemiah

1:3 "Those who survived the exile and are back in the province are in great trouble and disgrace. The wall of Jerusalem is broken down, and its gates have been burned with fire."

Nehemiah as Narrator

4 When I heard these things, I sat down and wept. For some days I mourned and fasted and prayed before the God of heaven.

Nehemiah to the Lord

5 "Lord, the God of heaven, the great and awesome God, who keeps his covenant of love with those who love him and keep his commandments, 6 let your ear be attentive and your eyes open to hear the prayer your servant is praying before you day and night for your servants, the people of Israel. I confess the sins we Israelites, including myself and my father's family, have committed against you… [11] *Lord, let your ear be attentive to the prayer of this your servant and to the prayer of your servants who delight in revering your name. Give your servant success today by granting him favor in the presence of this man.* [2:1] *I was cupbearer to the king.*

NEHEMIAH 1:3-6, 11; 2:1

Nehemiah as Narrator

[2:11] *I soon went to Jerusalem, and after staying there three days* [12] *I set out during the night with a few others. I had not told anyone what my God had put in my heart to do for Jerusalem. There were no mounts with me except the one I was riding on.* [13] *By night I went out through the Valley Gate toward the Jackal Well and the Dung Gate, examining the walls of Jerusalem, which had been broken down, and its gates, which had been destroyed by fire.* [16] *The officials did not know where I had gone or what I was doing, because as yet I had said nothing to the Jews or the priests or nobles or officials or any others who would be doing the work.*

Nehemiah to the Elders of Jerusalem

[17] *"You see the trouble we are in: Jerusalem lies in ruins, and its gates have been burned with fire. Come, let us rebuild the wall of Jerusalem, and we will no longer be in disgrace."* [18] *I also told them about the gracious hand of my God on me and what the king had said to me.*

Jerusalem Elders

"Let us start rebuilding."

NEHEMIAH 2:11-13, 16-18

Nehemiah as Narrator

[3:14] *So they began this good work. The Dung Gate was repaired by Malkijah, son of Rekab, ruler of the district of Beth Hakkerem. He rebuilt it and put its doors with their bolts and bars in place.* [23] *Beyond them, Benjamin and Hasshub made repairs in front of their house; and next to them, Azariah, son of Maaseiah, the son of Ananiah, made repairs beside his house.* [28] *Above the Horse Gate, the priests made repairs, each in front of his own house.* [32] *And between the room above the corner and the Sheep Gate, the goldsmiths and merchants made repairs.*

NEHEMIAH 3:14, 23, 28, 32

Sanballat

2 "What are those feeble Jews doing? Will they restore their wall? Will they offer sacrifices? Will they finish in a day? Can they bring the stones back to life from those heaps of rubble—burned as they are?"

Tobiah the Ammonite

3 "What they are building—even a fox climbing up on it would break down their wall of stones!"

Israelites

4 "Hear us, our God, for we are despised. Turn their insults back on their heads. Give them over as plunder in a land of captivity."

Nehemiah

13 Therefore, I stationed some people behind the lowest points of the wall at the exposed places, posting them by families, with their swords, spears, and bows. 14 After I looked things over, I stood up and said to the nobles, the officials, and the rest of the people, "Don't be afraid of them. Remember the Lord, who is great and awesome. Fight for your families, your sons and your daughters, your wives, and your homes."

NEHEMIAH 4:1-4, 13-14

THE BIGGER STORY

Comparing Nehemiah and Jesus as Leaders

Jesus, the greatest leader ever, naturally modeled many of Nehemiah's best traits: He felt deep compassion for his people's pains, founded his ministry activity in seasons of prayer, lived among the people he sought to serve, delegated the work that needed to be done, and embraced the reality of his ministry's opposition.

However, Jesus' leadership went a step further than Nehemiah's:

- ▶ He not only delegated leadership but reproduced himself in the lives of twelve apprentices.

- ▶ He loved his human "enemies" while confronting the true, unseen enemy head-on.

- ▶ He led with a divine level of authority and power, fully indwelt by God's Spirit.

Live into the Story

God the Hero

Because Nehemiah is like us, made in God's image, we know that whatever leadership traits we admire in him already exist in God. Reflect now on the Old Testament (OT) lessons you have experienced and other OT stories you may know. Pick one of the three God categories below of what Nehemiah also did. Then brainstorm several examples in each category.

► God grieving:

_____

_____

_____

► God delegating:

_____

_____

_____

► God overcoming Israel's enemies:

_____

_____

_____

Our Story

Recall the leadership traits and skills Nehemiah demonstrated in this lesson: prayer and compassion for those he would serve, listening to the people well, building a team, delegating the work, and overcoming opposition. Pick one of these traits where you want to grow as a leader. Explain how and why.

_____

_____

_____

_____

_____

Reaching Others

Review your response regarding the **What is Your Experience** question, then pick one place in your community needing leadership to "rebuild the broken walls." Name several actions and decisions a modern Nehemiah could make in that situation. Please explain.

_____

_____

_____

_____

Close Together in Prayer

Looking Ahead

After Nehemiah dies, God's people in Jerusalem again fall away from the Lord, his law, and their promises. A period of enemy oppression follows, mingled with a long season of God's silence—no prophets speak, no kings rule, and no judges come to rescue. This is God's dramatic pause before the Kingdom Story's climax: the triumphant introduction on earth of the long-awaited Messiah King, Jesus Christ.

Continue on with Lessons 11-20 in the *Kingdom Story Experience Small Group Study: New Testament.*

Prayer Ideas

▸ Thank the Lord for his servant Nehemiah and for Christ's even better example of a transforming leader.

▸ Be grateful for how you may *already* speak, act, and lead like Nehemiah.

▸ Ask God for his power to help you discern a new leadership step.

Action Ideas

▸ Name one leadership trait of Nehemiah you would like to model in your life. Come up with one action you can do to practice that trait this week in your community, workplace, or school. Be specific. Tell someone, then ask for their prayer.

Discipleship Practice

▸ **Leadership |** Leadership is the ability of a person to influence another or a group of people toward a challenging goal through motivating, modeling, mobilizing, and mentoring. *Why?* God is our ultimate leader but has delegated his power and designed humans to need visible leaders.

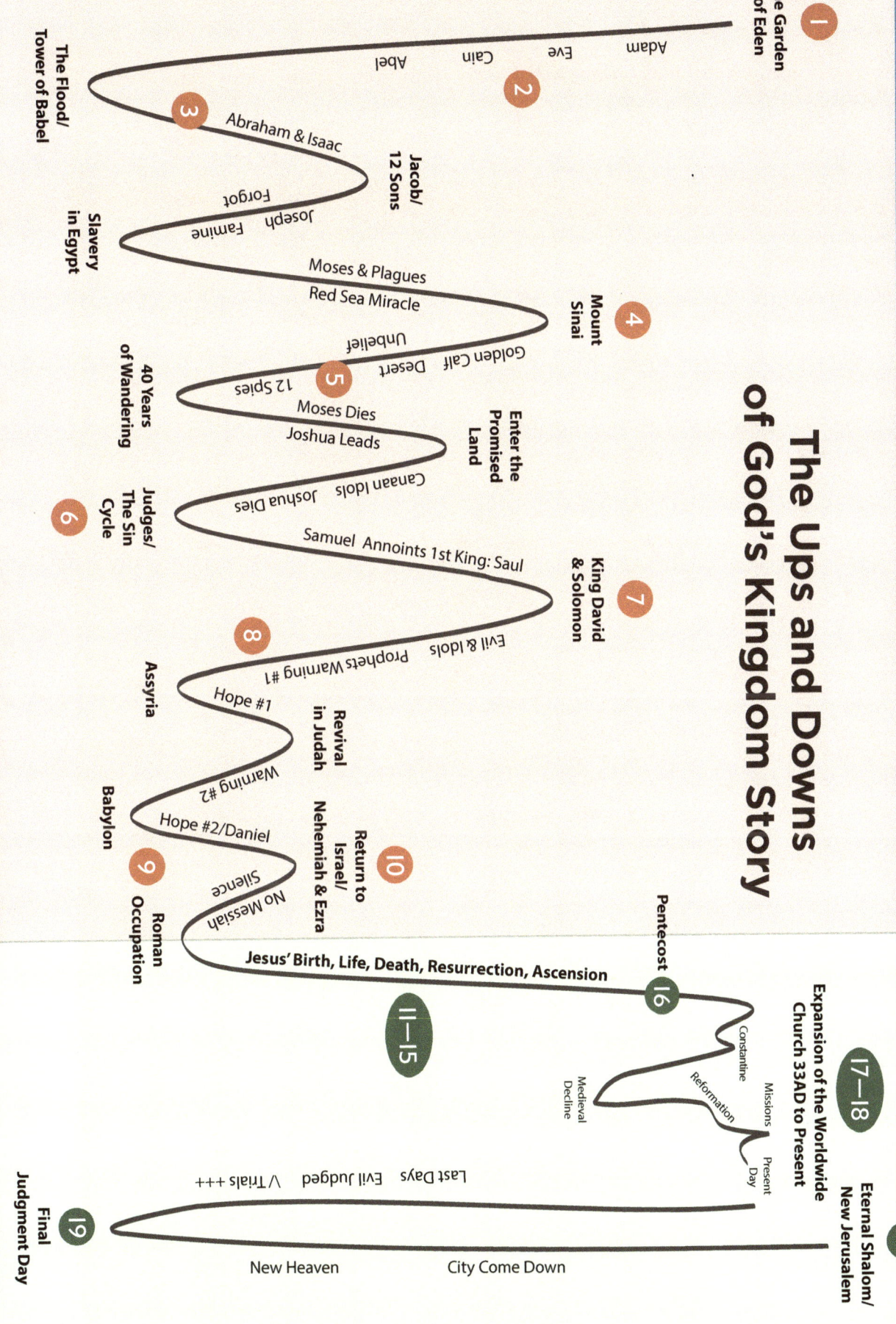

The Ups and Downs of God's Kingdom Story

OLD TESTAMENT

NEW TESTAMENT

1 The Garden of Eden

2 Adam • Eve • Cain • Abel

3 The Flood/ Tower of Babel • Abraham & Isaac

Jacob/ 12 Sons • Forgot • Famine • Joseph • Slavery in Egypt

4 Moses & Plagues • Red Sea Miracle • Mount Sinai

5 Golden Calf • Desert • Unbelief • 12 Spies • 40 Years of Wandering • Moses Dies • Joshua Leads • Enter the Promised Land

6 Canaan Idols • Joshua Dies • Judges/ The Sin Cycle

7 Samuel Annoints 1st King: Saul • King David & Solomon

8 Evil & Idols • Prophets Warning #1 • Assyria • Hope #1

Revival in Judah • Warning #2 • Babylon • Hope #2/Daniel

9 Silence • No Messiah • Roman Occupation

10 Return to Israel/ Nehemiah & Ezra

11—15 Jesus' Birth, Life, Death, Resurrection, Ascension

16 Pentecost

Expansion of the Worldwide Church 33AD to Present • Constantine • Medieval Decline • Reformation • Missions Day • Present Day

17—18

20 Eternal Shalom/ New Jerusalem

19 Final Judgment Day • Last Days • Evil Judged • √ Trials +++ • New Heaven • City Come Down

Acknowledgments

Every book requires a host of helpers, but a workbook facilitating a participatory experience of discipleship takes my indebtedness to a higher level.

The Kingdom Story Experience *is just that, an experience that has involved groups since 1994, people of many ages and several nationalities. Trial and error, drafts and redrafts, happened continuously over the last three decades; every group of these yearly experiences has in its own way helped me shape what you will find in this material. There have been no lack of honest critics and cheerleaders along the way. It has taken a village.*

Another collage of friends and strategic partners have taken time to edit, rewrite, type set, and give me important feedback over the last 4 decades: Paul Allen, Jen Dean, Levi Edgecombe, Matt Allen, Arthur Koh, Arlyn Lawerence, Cody Lail, Andrew Hilzendeger, Denee Curl, Jennifer Tabert, and Connie Willems, and I am sure I have forgotten a few.

Two people stand out: many long, honest conversations and thoughtful feedback with co-teacher Branden Hubbell have brought the KSE to a sharper focus it so desperately needed. Kami Wright took on the project of a modern re-design and spent hours working on artwork, formatting, and taking in my incessant "last-minute" edits—and all with good cheer and encouragement! Branden and Kami's contributions have proved valuable beyond measure.

I am most indebted to my living King Jesus Christ. This publication is to me a living reminder of God's faithfulness to weave together some of the messy, miraculous, and mundane stories of my ministry years. Teaching The Kingdom Story Way *(the first iteration of what you hold now) has been, I must admit, in no small part selfish; it is hard to imagine my life apart from being tethered, again and again and again, to Christ's Spirit through the people and experiences of The Kingdom Story.*

— John

www.ingramcontent.com/pod-product-compliance
Lightning Source LLC
Chambersburg PA
CBHW041120120626
46547CB00019B/2780